"BOOM Thinking is just what we all need! From the very beginning, Cheri is urging us to blow up our worlds as we know them – a radical thought in the traditional self help movement which encourages bigger and better, but not blowing it up and starting over. She speaks directly to you – not to your brain, but to your heart and that little part inside that knows what's really going on and has been waiting for some help to get you to see all the hooey you've been telling yourself. You know from the very first chapter this is something that will shake things up, and shake them up for good. It's Big, Bold, and Booming. I can't believe Cheri has been holding out on us for so long…she was born to share this message!"

Nina East, IAC-CC
Author, *Rapid Relationship Recovery*
Founder, The Association of Personal Growth Professionals
www.PersonalGrowthProfessionals.com

"Insightful, inspirational, and informative. Cheri's process takes the best of successful strategies, and delivers them with clarity and a great sense of humor while targeting the biggest obstacle to our own happiness; ourselves. A must read for anyone wanting the best out of business, life, and love."

Robert P. Jacoby, M.S., LPC, NCC
Psychotherapist, Author of *Gamemaster*

"In a perfect world, everyone would be willing to share the trials as well as the triumphs of their lives, for the sake of helping each other. As it is, we are fortunate that Cheri is not only willing to do so, but able to in a way that is refreshingly authentic. Her advice for change is so wonderfully accessible; she is to be commended for clearing the way to a more purposeful life for anyone who is ready to make these all-important shifts."

Jenifer Madson, Financial Success Coach
Author of *A FINANCIAL MINUTE: From Money Madness to Financial Freedom, One Minute at a Time*
www.afinancialminute.com

"A few days after reading Cheri's book I used it in a session with a client. Why? Because her approach is vivid, fresh, and practical. If you are looking for a motivational kickstart, this is a good one."

Molly Gordon, Master Coach
Author of *The Way of the Accidental Entrepreneur: How to Grow a Business that Fits Just-Right and Authentic Promotion: Grow Your Business, Feed Your Soul*
www.mollygordon.com.

"Cheri Britton's BOOM Thinking approach is a witty, wise and wonderful way to tackle the tough changes and rough patches that are part of life. Candid, humorous and authentic, Cheri holds up the mirror to help you see where you're holding yourself back and what's sucking the life out of your living. More importantly, Cheri's BOOM Thinking approach gives you the mental dynamite to blast those suckers right off your planet. This book is so full of Cheri's energy and personality, it's like having her over for coffee. So get gutsy and start booming!"

Gail Martin, President, DreamSpinner Communications
Host, Shared Dreams Marketing Podcast
Author, *The Chronicles of the Necromancer series*
www.DreamSpinnerCommunications.com

BOOM

Thinking

CHERI BRITTON, M.ED.

BOOM Thinking

THE GUTSY GUIDE TO BREAKING OUT OF OLD MINDSETS

Copyright © 2008 by Cheri Britton

Illustrations by Moni Hill
Cover Design by Kara Brown
Text Design by Cheri Britton
Typography by Michelle Brown

ISBN 0-7414-4618-9

Published by:

1094 New DeHaven Street, Suite 100
West Conshohocken, PA 19428-2713
Info@buybooksontheweb.com
www.buybooksontheweb.com
Toll-free (877) BUY BOOK
Local Phone (610) 941-9999
Fax (610) 941-9959

Printed in the United States of America
Printed on Recycled Paper
Published June 2008

To my kids, daughter Sawyer and son Noah,
who show me daily that
perfection comes in many guises.

I love you very much!

The Gutsy Guide to Breaking Out of Old Mindsets

Table of Contents

Acknowledgments

To my editor, Jonna Rae Bartges, who made words dance and ideas flow; to dear friend Katherine Daven, who always encouraged me and kept Sasha in line; to treasured curmudgeon Bill Petz, who critically scrutinized each word and weeded out the woo-woo; to friend and confidante Jeanne McGowan, whose constant optimism brought sunshine to my stormiest days; to artist and friend Moni Hill for illustrating my dreams; and to my wonderful assistant Stefanie Beierschmitt, who kept the business humming while I was immersed in outlines and deadlines, thank you.

I want to thank all the people I've met or coached through the years and all the coaches who have guided me, especially Jennifer Louden, Nina East, and Isabel Parlett, and all the friends and clients who kept saying, "So, when's your book coming out?" Guilt is a marvelous motivator.

This book wouldn't have been possible without the help of consultant Brenda Dahmann, Alexandra and Peter ter Horst, who helped me crystalize the language for BOOM Thinking, or my Gelt Girlfriends, who each supported me and my business with her special expertise: Totsie Marine, Ginger Graziano, Melissa Stantz, Linda Brandt and Elizabeth Barbour. Also, my gratitude to Kara Brown for weaving Moni's illustrations and my ideas into one colorful coherent cover; and to Michelle Brown for making each page picture perfect.

Thanks to Lori Aszman for always being there with a quick "Atta girl!" and Monica Thomas for her eternal enthusiasm for my work.

Special thanks to Diane English, Tena Frank, Lynne Harty, Patricia Dee, Julie Parker, Sandi Tomlin-Sutker, Ana Tampana, Lincoln Crum, Caren Olmsted, Mary Beth Kingston and Robin Payne for allowing me to share their stories with you in this book.

Finally, I'd like to express heartfelt gratitude to everyone on the home front — my kids, Sawyer and Noah; Chris Britton, the nicest ex-husband (or "was-band") a woman could have; my mother, Jan Dunn, and my late stepfather, Paul Dunn; my father and stepmother, Dan and Eunice Goodwin, my brother Chris Goodwin and his wife Karen, and my K-9 Corps, Chance, Moxie and Boomer. I love you all!

FOREWORD
BY JENNIFER LOUDEN

*C*heri is one of those people who can't help but "motivate people to change for the better." She asks the hard questions: How can we keep waking up to the miracle of this moment and the miracle we are? How can we continue to allow life to inspire and fill us, to move us? These questions are some of the most important we can contemplate in our life, and they are addressed with such humor and grit in this book.

How we think and *what* we think directly shape what we believe is possible. That's been the message of saints and sages for as long as we have written records. It's the foundation that makes all other teachings, like love thy neighbor and don't litter, possible. The ancient Vedic scriptures preached this message – so did Buddha and Jesus. Now we have Oprah carrying the good news… and Cheri! Perhaps this awareness is gaining such momentum and media because it's central to our survival as a species. I can just imagine God kvetching, "How much louder and clearer can I make it? How come they don't get it?" Well, no worries – Cheri's here to bring the message home.

Cheri's words are a direct transmission of her questing spirit.

Simply reading her story will help you break free from fusty mindsets and shed the obstacles concealing your natural brilliance—it's like one of those magic diet pills we read about in the back pages of *Parade* magazine, only this one really works. And if you are willing to roll up your sleeves and do a few of her exercises, you're going to blind yourself with your shining clarity, your innate genius and the profound truth that you always have within you exactly what you need.

Get ready to rock your world.

Jennifer Louden
Bainbridge Island, Washington 2008

Editor's Note: Jennifer Louden is a best-selling author, life coach and social commentator. Her works include the popular Women's Comfort series of books and the newly released The Life Organizer: A Women's Guide to a Mindful Year.
www.jenniferlouden.com

Introduction

Before I sat down to write this introduction for the book that has been simmering on my back burner for years, I took a friend's black lab for a walk. The North Carolina night sky was peppered with stars, and Bear and I stopped to oooww and ahh. Countless stars represented billions of gallaxies, with who knows how much intelligent life. It made me stop and think — my book and I were both faint, inconsequential blips on the radar of reality.

As I was asking myself, "Who am I to think I have something new to offer people in a self-help book?" I was reminded of the words of my coach and friend, Nina East. She said, "Even though it's been said before, there will be people who will hear this message *best* coming from you."

The process of changing from the limiting way things were to the more positive way they will be certainly isn't new, and I don't pretend to have invented it. That's precisely why this book was a decade in the making.

Who was I to think I had something different to share with people who feel "stuck" in their lives? Aren't there enough of these books already? My fears of being redundant or, worse, *presumptious* effectively created a metaphoric cement wall between me and a completed book. The only thing I could offer was a process I created that guides people in confronting limiting beliefs and overcoming them. The more I thought about all the reasons I couldn't write the book, the more I put the process to work and created compelling reasons for why I *could*. You're holding the proof that BOOM Thinking works — I finally wrote the darn thing.

In all seriousness, this book is the culmination of a lifetime of discovery, hard knocks, heartbreak and joy. Yes, bookstore shelves are crammed with self-help books, but this is *my* story, *my* life, *my* labor of love to help people get real with themselves and sacrifice the known comfort of a velvet rut for the exhilarating possibility of living life on all cylinders.

Because BOOM Thinking has worked for so many clients and businesses through the years, I wanted to share it with a wider audience. Just as I ask of the people I instruct in the transformational process of BOOM Thinking, I want you to make a commitment to do some serious work on yourself. You're going to need a journal, a pen, and a good dose of courage.

The people we bring into our lives are effective mirrors, making us reflect on our own accomplishments or failings as we take note of theirs. In the same way, writing down deep inner thoughts that are much more comfortably ignored will mirror back to us who we truly are, and why. That's why exercises at the end of each chapter in this book challenge you to journal your answers to probing questions. Each chapter builds upon the next, with the exercises designed to gradually put you in touch with the real you. If you take the time to answer the questions honestly, I promise you, you will transform your belief systems and rock your world.

Like there are countless stars in the night skies, there are countless processes to make your life count for something great. Maybe, just maybe, BOOM Thinking will be yours. Now, let's start your transformation.

All the best,
Cheri

"*You can't solve a problem with the same mind that created it.*"

~*Albert Einstein*

An Invitation to Blow Up Your World as You Know It

Chapter 1

Chapter 1

An Invitation to Blow Up Your World as You Know It

You know the feeling — work is going all right, you're reasonably comfortable in your relationship with a significant other, family communication is happening on a relatively regular basis, and while not perfect, your health is OK, too. All the important areas of your routine are right about average.

But then, "life" happens.

This reality that was fitting you like a comfortable old glove begins to pinch a bit. You're passed over for that anticipated promotion. You and your spouse start to bicker over minor stuff.

The kids seem to have sprouted horns and fangs overnight. And those favorite pants shrank in the dryer. Again. (Darn dryer!)

Suddenly, your life is *not* OK, and you realize, in hindsight, that you have "settled" for an average existence while your unpursued dreams are burning a hole in your heart. The most dangerous thing about living in a velvet rut is most people don't even realize they're in one until the day they wake up and say, "What happened to me? Why am I so unhappy?"

The wonderful thing about reaching this state of mental, physical and/or spiritual pain is *now* you're motivated to shift things around, to flush out the gunk that's holding you back and reclaim your passion for life.

Welcome to BOOM Thinking!

The Velvet Rut:

You will read this term many times throughout this book. It's probably a familiar feeling. You are snuggled down on the couch, watching your favorite TV show (for me it is CSI reruns) and you are drifting off to sleep. You know you should get up, brush your teeth, wash your face, turn out the lights and go to bed like a *mature* adult. But you feel soooooo good where you are. Your heart rate has slowed; you are so warm and cozy on the sofa. You think to yourself, "Well, just a few more minutes."

But you don't get up. You stay in that soft cocoon on the sofa only to wake up at 2:42 a.m. with Jerry Springer on the TV, a sticky, bad-tasting film on your teeth and a wrench in your neck. You want to kick yourself for not getting up and going to bed hours ago. You are now paying the cost of allowing your momentary comfort to lure you into ignoring your oh-so-wise self.

Now mind you, I've never done this (oh, get real). In truth, I know all too well the irritated feeling I get when I realize that I've allowed my "comfort" to keep me from doing what was actually best for me. This is what I call **The Velvet Rut.** (I first heard these words uttered by a beloved Solopreneur woman coaching client and I thought they were brilliant… so I, of course, stole them!)

The **Velvet Rut** is that place of comfort we reside in when we are doing one of two things: 1) Engaging in some comforting behavior that is ultimately against our goals, or 2) Avoiding doing something that would be uncomfortable for us at the onset but is in our overall best interest.

For example, we may be continuing to shop, piling up debt because it's just so darn fun AND "It's such a great deal!" We stay in that comfortable place of denial about our money situation while we live it up with new shoes, dinners out and a whole new skin care line. Or another popular example: we avoid establishing an exercise routine because we know that those first few weeks of getting into the groove are pretty darn hard — not only physically, but mentally as well. So we don't exercise and instead decide to stay in that comfortable place of inaction.

But continuing to shop and avoiding exercise keep us in the **Velvet Rut.** We allow ourselves to stay on that warm and snuggly metaphorical sofa. Remaining in the **Velvet Rut** allows us to avoid the undeniable discomfort that comes when we shift our behavior, even a shift that would be for our own good.

But just like we know that we will pay when we remain on the sofa past our bedtime, there is a part of us that knows that overspending or remaining sedentary will, at some point, have a cost, too. Eventually, the credit card bills will arrive or our jeans will get more snug. Sooner or later, we will want to kick our own butt for not accepting the **healthy discomfort** of making choices that ultimately support our best interests.

Here is how the BOOM process works:

First, Put on the Brakes!!

What's the major limiting belief in your life at this very moment that's holding you back from where you want to be? If you're really good at self flagellation, you have a whole warehouse full of them. For this exercise, just pick the surliest, most threatening and overwhelming one. Got it? Are you feeling uncomfortable just thinking about it? Great! That's EXACTLY what we're going for!

Until you're in serious discomfort with a situation, behavior or thought, you'll just keep adjusting and plodding along in that same rut, the way you might not immediately stop to take a pebble out of your shoe during a long hike. Frequently, it's not until that pebble has made each step pure agony that you'll be motivated to stop, unlace your hiking boot, shake out the offender and rub that tender spot on the bottom of your foot. I want you to feel so terrible that you just can't bear to take one more step in a world where this limiting belief has such power over you. Until you reach that tipping point, you're not really ready to change anyway.

> *Pack your own parachute.*
>
> ~ T.L.Hakala

Then, Observe

Now, let's take a look at this bad boy. Where did this limiting belief come from? When did it first latch on to your self-esteem? Did someone say or do something to you at some point in your life, or is this a self-imposed roadblock?

We drag so many hurtful memories from childhood with us and frequently never make the connection that we're still giving these shadows from the past such power over us. For instance, one of my college professors told me, repeatedly, that I wasn't a writer. Decades later, when I was still too intimidated to plunk myself down at my keyboard and start writing this book, I suddenly realized — "This is just NUTS! I'm smarter than this! I can DO this!" It took some work, but eventually, I could let that old belief go.

Once you've identified where the darn thing came from, you can start figuring out why, on either a conscious or subconscious level, you accepted it in the first place. How has this belief been protecting you? How does claiming it benefit you?

What do you NOT have to do as long as this limiting belief dominates you? What will you sacrifice if you release it? What new responsibilities or expectations will you have when you *do* blow it out of your life?

Take some time with this step, and be honest. It can go pretty deep. In fact, in my years of helping people BOOM Think, I've seen over and over again how these limiting beliefs usually have VERY deep roots.

Now, Obliterate!

Here comes the fun part — blow that sucker up. Literally see this limiting belief being blasted to smithereens, relinquishing all of its power over you and your emotions.

I've had people get creative and imagine the old issue being wired with explosives and then imploding in on itself with a dramatic Ka-BOOM and a cloud of smoke. Some people imagine it being consumed in cleansing flames.

For those who are more mellow, simply see this limiting belief being gently dissolved into light. Thank it for whatever positive function it fulfilled in the past and confirm it is time for it to move on.

Whatever your preferred method of visual clearing and release, GO for it. This old way of thinking and being is no longer serving you. It's gotta go.

NOW. *BOOM* that thing!

Finally, Make a New Mindset

At this point, you've done the hard work of dislodging an old belief that no longer served you. Now you get to be creative. Nature abhors a vacuum, so create a positive, powerful new thought or behavior to take the place of the one you just obliterated.

A note of caution here — you must be honest with yourself. If you're seriously tone-deaf and you try to tell yourself you're going to BOOM Think your way to singing like Josh Grobin or Celine Dion, your "inner critic" will instantly respond with a hearty, "You are SO full of it!" As you create this powerful, positive new mindset, make sure it's firmly grounded in reality. We'll talk a *lot* more about inner critics and their purpose in your life in Chapter Four.

When I finally decided to BOOM Think that professor's put-down about my supposed lack of writing ability, I reminded myself that I was actually quite the little communicator. I was in demand as a speaker, I created information-filled handouts for my clients, and I had even written several education curriculums. In fact, I finally realized, I was a talented and interesting writer! Armed with this very accurate assessment of my personal strengths, it was easy for me to consciously accept the fact that writing was no longer this ominous, amorphous thing that could suck all logic and order from my brain cells. I trusted the validity of this new mindset, that I was actually quite good at juggling words. I could easily write regular columns for the local newspaper and put the heart of the message I shared with businesses, groups and individuals into a pithy, practical book. That's why the positive new mindset worked. It was firmly rooted in reality.

Change your mindset and change your life. It sounds simple, but you know it's not.

Change is scary as all get-out, and like we've discussed, it's usually not a comfortable process. If you're reading this book, chances are there's something, or a nest of somethings, eating away at you. You have grown weary of struggling to merely stay afloat, and you're ready to reclaim your throne and scepter as Master of Your Universe.

> *The most important thing about getting somewhere is starting right where we are.*
>
> *~ Bruce Barton*

So, here's my invitation. If you're truly ready to make a sincere effort to change your life for the better, BOOM Thinking will be your life raft in a sea of deep issues (or box of tissues!). If, however, someone *gave* you this book, you might want to just close it right now and check out something good on cable. Change is not easy, and it's not for sissies. It has to be something YOU want to do for YOU, not for your significant other, parents, kids, boss or other demanding external dominating force, real or imagined. All your "putting on the brakes, observing, obliterating and building new mindsets" has to come from within you or it will have the permanence of an exquisite outdoor ice sculpture on a July day in Death Valley.

You're going to have to make a commitment and get your brain around the concept that you have options and that you're making a vow to discover and embrace them.

At the end of this work, you're going to be a completely different person. I'm not saying you should stop seeing your therapist if you have one — I LOVE therapists! (mine's on speed dial) — but get ready for some big changes that you're about to initiate in your life.

Here's another quick reality check to see if you're actually ready to rock your world:

The three things new BOOM Thinkers have in common are:

1. They define themselves as **being "stuck"** in some area of their life.
2. On some level, they know **things can be better** than they are.
3. The pain has gotten so unbearable **they're finally reaching out** for help.

The three things they have in common *after* doing BOOM Thinking are:

1. Suddenly, they discover **they have way more options** than they thought were possible. Even if they thought *maybe* they had one or two, the BOOM Thinking process puts them in touch with many positive new ways of being.
2. BOOM Thinkers **feel the power** in simply allowing themselves to be in a place of self-awareness. It's validating and nourishing on mental, physical, emotional and spiritual levels.
3. People who sincerely do the BOOM Thinking process begin to develop an optimistic realization that **the pain that's motivating them to change is *not* the way it's going to be**. They shift one thing in their life, and the pieces start to fall into place like dominoes. There's a positive momentum that's triggered when you take the first conscious steps towards healing your life.

Sound good? Then let's get BOOMin'!

Exercises

1. What is the one major limiting belief that, if it were gone, would make your life different? In my experience, the first thing that comes to your mind is usually not the most limiting belief. Do a brain dump on this. Most of us have a bunch of hot buttons in various areas of our lives, for instance:

   Relationships; Money; Family; Health; Body Image; Career; Creativity; Power; Love; Politics; Aging; Spirituality/Religion.

   Did you flinch on any of these? Great! Write down the first things that came to your mind for each of them. You'll be getting closer to honestly pinpointing the monsters in your metaphorical closet. Listening to your gut is an important part of getting real with yourself and becoming a successful BOOM Thinker.

2. Take an inventory. Here's where you get to do another brain dump. Begin with the past month. Write down 10 things you accomplished. Cast a wide net here. Even what you might at first glance see as an insignificant thing, like recycling household paper and plastics, is a positive step.

3. Once you've made that list, keep going. List 10 things you've accomplished in the past year. Then do a list of 10 things you've done over the past five years.

Hold on to these lists. You'll be using these insights in the next few chapters.

"The truth is that our finest moments are most likely to occur when we are feeling deeply uncomfortable, unhappy, or unfulfilled. For it is only in such moments, propelled by our discomfort, that we are likely to step out of our ruts and start searching for different ways or truer answers."

~ M.Scott Peck

The Birth of BOOM Thinking

Chapter 2

Chapter Two

The Birth of BOOM Thinking

You know how they always say, "You teach best what you most need to learn?" So true, my friends. Sooooo true.

A handful of years ago, I was puttering along in my life, making pretty good time but having no idea where I was headed. My husband accepted a new job in Asheville, North Carolina, so we pulled up our Charlotte roots and headed west. My marriage seemed fine, and I'd been using my Masters degree in Health Education to educate thousands of people about sexuality, but I still had the vague, unsettled feeling that this vanilla existence just wasn't "enough."

I was aimlessly browsing in a bookstore when a slim purple volume literally fell on my left foot. "**Comfort Secrets for Busy Women: Finding Your Way When Your Life Is Overflowing** by Jennifer Louden," I read aloud. Who knew that guardian angels were such good little personal shoppers?

Of course I devoured Jennifer's wise and eclectic thoughts on "The Nudge We Need to Create Our Lives," crooked thinking and "it is what it is." She challenged, inspired and…well…*comforted* me with her words, so I hired her as my very first coach. With her wisdom, humor and encouragement, Jennifer helped me unearth what else I needed to have in my life — I needed an audience! While one-on-one coaching was and continues to be an important and rewarding part of my life, there's just something about sharing with a crowd that nourishes my very soul. This was what I had been searching for!

Soon, various groups in the area were engaging me as an inspirational speaker. While Jennifer catapulted me into this new arena, I didn't stop there. As more people met me through my presentations, they began asking me to coach them. My years of experience as a counselor had fine-tuned my abilities to guide others personally and professionally, and that part of my life began to flourish, too.

Sounds good, right? It was — to a degree.

Despite the way things were beginning to take off for me, I realized I needed some help in focusing on exactly what it was that I did. I was trying to reconcile my health consulting business, my speaking engagements and my business coaching. It felt like I was trying to compare apples and oranges and pears. I needed to be able to say authentically what I did, not "in this part of my life I do this, and in this part of my life I do this." I needed a solid base from which to launch the rest of my professional career.

> *What keeps you going isn't some fine destination, but just the road you're on, and the fact that you know how to drive.*
>
> ~ Barbara Kingsolver

Enter Isabel!

After two years of struggling with how to tell people what I did, I registered for a National Speakers Association conference in Phoenix with a mixture of anticipation and dread. I knew I'd meet interesting people, but I also knew I'd be asked, repeatedly, to describe my business. During one of the session breaks I met a pleasant woman and casually asked her what *she* did. Her response was so crystal clear, engaging and enthusiastic that I spontaneously clutched her arm and exclaimed, "You just rocked my world!"

She laughed and said, "I just learned how to talk about myself from my incredible coach, Isabel Parlett. And you won't believe it, but her tagline is 'helping you find the words to rock their world!'"

Ah — Earth to Cheri? It was definitely another sign!

Of course I hired Isabel Parlett to help me gain some clarity. She began by asking me what it is I naturally do well. I'm willing to bet you've never really pondered that, either. It was a fascinating inner journey. What I eventually realized is that I naturally do a *variety* of things well.

- I'm very comfortable sharing my truths with others.
- I question what some people say to be true.
- I'm comfortable with seeing things as gray, not just black or white.
- I'm comfortable with saying things can change.
- I'm a catalyst who motivates people to change for the better.

I didn't have the language at the time, but what Isabel helped me realize is that for years I was DARN good at helping people break out of their old mindsets about sexuality and HIV. I was able to help them see that they *could* change their lives and get off of drugs or establish safer sexual behaviors.

In the same way, I could motivate business people to change how they ran their company, help them build it into the successful, focused organization they desired it to be.

Those same powerful, positive techniques I used to motivate and inspire the HIV patients and business clients also lit a fire under audiences at speaking engagements. A little humor, a lot of truth, and — BOOM! Some amazing transformations began to happen as people wrapped their brains around the liberating idea that they had *options*. They could *change* the things they didn't want in their lives anymore. They could *shift* their concept of themselves, their behaviors and most of all, those beliefs that, in the past, had limited them.

BOOM Thinking is Born

In defining those things I just couldn't stop myself from doing, I was thrilled to discover the very things that defined me and brought me joy through accomplishing them. I realized that guiding people through changing their old beliefs was the thread that tied together all the jobs in my life that, on the surface, seemed so disparate.

> *It is not the strongest of the species that survives, nor the most intelligent, but the one most responsive to change.*
>
> *~ Charles Darwin*

The actual name for this entire process — BOOM Thinking — was created as I was considering how to market my unique talent to move people forward.

Isabel noted that I had a booming voice and personality. Guilty!

> *The turning point in the process of growing up is when you discover the core strength within you.*
>
> ~ Max Lerner

Some friends have charitably described me as "a party waiting to happen." The words "shy and reserved" are not in my vocabulary, thank you very much! Speaking in front of a big group, the number one fear in the nation, is my catnip.

As I was ruminating on a suitable term for what I had to offer, Alexandra ter Horst, an Asheville publicist, commented on a candid picture of me hugging my lovable mutt. "I just love this shot of you and Boomer," she said. "You know, the word 'Boom' seems to personify you." Ding! Ding! Ding! We had a WINNER! The Universal Voice of Coincidental Solutions had spoken. "BOOM Thinking" it was!

Now that I had the perfect name, I set about creating the acronym that would accurately explain it. It was as if it was suddenly spelled out in colored lights — **B**reak **O**ut of **O**ld **M**indsets.

Although it seemed like I was working backwards from there, I created the four specific steps in the BOOM process, making sure each emphasized the corresponding letter: Put on the <u>B</u>rakes, <u>O</u>bserve what is happening, <u>O</u>bliterate what no longer works for you, <u>M</u>ake a new Mindset.

Finding My Path

Even though this was a rather unorthodox order for creating the name for my work, I felt very confident that it truly came from what Cheri Britton does best. What is my mission? What do I believe I need to do? Because it was created that way -- it was organic and kind of kitschy – it felt much more authentic to me. I had my focus!

It wasn't like I tried to think of something the world needed, and then created it. You know, like "People are carrying cell phones and need a little bag to hook them to their purse." I didn't do that. Instead, with Isabel's help, I was able to focus on what I already felt called to do. I gave it a memorable name, and a graphic look.

While I was so relieved to be bringing my work into focus, my own limiting mind had a field day. My merciless inner critic, who's waiting to meet you in Chapter Four, whispered in my ear, "Who are *you* to tell people how to break out of old mindsets when you're still struggling?"

At first the accusation stung, but as I BOOMED it, I understood its purpose.

Struggling but Successful

YES, I'm still struggling with some limiting beliefs. For instance, some days I berate myself that I haven't fit into a size 4 since I got my clothes in the Macys Toddler section. But while I'm struggling with some emotional roadblocks, I've been quite successful with blowing many others up and achieving numerous goals that have helped me help others.

In our society, we value pluckiness — the refusal to immediately say "Uncle!" even when it seems a sumo wrestler has us in a headlock.

> *There is a microscopically thin line between being brilliantly creative and acting like the most gigantic idiot on earth. So what the hell, leap.*
>
> ~ Cynthia Heimel

"Struggling but successful" *works*. Look at venerable funny man Robin Williams, who always bounces back from box office bombs. (Did ANYONE see *License to Wed*?) Katie Couric was bounced from an on-air reporting gig at CNN because her bosses decided "she wasn't ready for a big audience," and promptly claimed the top spot on The Today Show for 15 years (and many millions of dollars).

My personal favorite example of both BOOM Thinking and "struggling but successful" is megastar Oprah Winfrey. This remarkable woman didn't fit society's stereotypical ideas of "beauty" when she launched her TV career as a reporter at the tender age of 19. Even after claiming her place in history as broadcasting pioneer, billionaire and master influencer of public opinion, she continues to struggle with her weight, being abused as a child, and most recently, sexual transgressions by one of the employees at her groundbreaking school for girls in Africa. Even though she called that revelation one of the most painful things

> *One is not born, but rather becomes a woman.*
>
> *~ Simone de Beauvoir*

she's ever endured, we know this magnificent woman immediately put on the brakes, observed how this could have happened, obliterated the old system that put an alleged child molester on the payroll, and created a new mindset and a new policy for hiring practices at the school. She also immediately provided all of the students with cell phones to personally contact her in an emergency.

We probably wouldn't love Oprah the way we do if she never suffered. It makes her human, and it makes us cheer her successes all the more. We feel like she's real — she's one of *us*. She's had her share of knocks, but she refuses to stay down. She owns the bad, like chiding herself for the day she pulled a wagon of fat out on stage to celebrate that temporary weight loss years back. Her authenticity and perseverance inspire and motivate us. When she suggests we read or try something, we're *there*.

In the same way that Oprah has used the pain in her life to move forward and inspire others, I believe the whole purpose of BOOM Thinking is to be realistic about what's not working for you, learn from it, and rework your life to eliminate the habits and behaviors that have, in the past, limited your success and happiness.

Exercises.

1. What do you naturally do well? Make a list.

2. What are the things you just can't help but do?

3. What are your passions?

4. What are the things that would make you ecstatic if you never had to do them again?

5. What things truly give your life meaning?

6. Go back over all the lists and mark the overlaps. What do these lists tell you?

"First you find out why it is that you may think the way you think and what conditions have arisen to make you feel that way, and then you find out how to change them."

~ Fred Alan Wolf, Ph.D.

The Science Behind BOOM Thinking

Chapter 3

Chapter 3

The Science Behind BOOM Thinking

For a great crash course in BOOM Thinking, I suggest you watch the science-meets-spirituality movie blockbuster, *What the Bleep Do We Know!?* This documentary took on the daunting task of explaining the link between quantum physics, Western medicine, theology and philosophy in layman's terms. It truly helped me understand how my emotions literally influence what's happening in my brain and body.

One of my favorite parts is an animated explanation of neurological receptors, the work of brilliant scientist/author/spiritualist Candace Pert, Ph.D. Dr. Pert's research proved that the more we experience a particular emotion, good *or* bad, the more we desire to repeat the experience. Our cells, she says, which are depicted as cartoony

> *Self-deception remains the most difficult deception. The tricks that work on others count for nothing in that very well lit back alley where one keeps assignations with oneself...*
>
> ~ Joan Didion

blobs with human features and frailties in the movie, literally create protein receptors on the surface which gobble up the chemicals we produce when we're happy, sad, aroused, desiring control – every emotion we experience. By extrapolation, we create both an emotional and physical dependence on the feelings that we consciously focus on the most.

When we stay in a constant state of feeling victimized, for instance, our cells sprout a ravenous covering of receptors craving the very specific proteins our body creates while in a state of low self-esteem. If and when we realize this is not an emotional state we wish to perpetuate, we not only have to change our external environment that's triggering that emotion — we have to change our cellular environment by shifting our response to that external stimulus. In other words, we must change the meaning we're giving to that thing or things that sabotaged our self-esteem in the first place.

In a nutshell, that's the scientific foundation behind the process of BOOM Thinking. To change your life, you have to change the way you think by building a new mindset. The only way to stop feeling scared or confused or angry or victimized is by starving those protein receptors that feed off of the chemicals we create when we're in a limiting state of mind. When we make that emotional shift to a more positive state, we produce different biochemicals and nurture protein receptors for joy, compassion, and fulfillment — all the good stuff we desire to increase in our lives.

Don't Worry, Be Happy! (SERIOUSLY!)

Two of the key reasons BOOM Thinking works so well are the process helps you develop the habit of creating a positive mental attitude without a false Pollyanna-like façade, and it also encourages you to write down your thoughts on various issues. In both regards, BOOM Thinking might be considered "Cognitive Behavioral Therapy — Lite!"

Instead of focusing on issues from early childhood, Cognitive Behavior Therapy focuses on how you're thinking, behaving and communicating *now*. You and your therapist work together to identify thoughts you want to change, and you do a series of homework assignments to help you shift your thinking and deal with real-life issues effectively.

Another branch of psychology takes the concept of working to shift into a positive mindset a step further. In *A Primer of Positive*

Psychology, Christopher Peterson, Ph.D., talks about the work he's done with Dr. Martin Seligman, director of the University of Pennsylvania Positive Psychology Center. Dr. Seligman is revered as the founder of Positive Psychology, a new branch, which focuses on what makes people happy and why. He has researched the effectiveness of "positive psychology interventions" for people who are chronically depressed, and his work was featured in the July/August 2007 issue of the *American Psychologist*, the journal of the American Psychology Association.

Under the direct supervision of Dr. Seligman, U of P now offers the first Master of Applied Positive Psychology program to train people to literally make the world a happier place.

While BOOM Thinking is certainly not a substitute for professional cognitive therapy if therapy is warranted, it *is* a powerful, effective process for helping people break out of a rut and shift into a more positive frame of mind. Please consult with a mental health professional any time you're feeling completely overwhelmed or hopeless.

Wheelbarrows Work, Too

While the animated blobs in *What the Bleep!?* are a great way to illustrate the science of BOOM Thinking, I also love to use the wheelbarrow metaphor. Imagine you've been pushing a wheelbarrow filled with wood from point A to point B for years. With each trip, that heavy wheelbarrow compacts the earth more and more until you wear a deep groove into your normal path. If you ever decide to deviate from your old pattern, it's going to take considerable effort to push the

> *Courage is the power to let go of the familiar.*
>
> ~ Raymond Linquist

heavy wheelbarrow out of the well-worn rut and in a new direction.

In a similar way, thinking the same thought or doing the same behavior repeatedly literally creates a physical neural network in the brain. It will take concentrated effort to obliterate that old neurological pathway and create a new thought pattern, but it can be done. BOOM Thinking helps you "rewire" your brain and get out of the metaphorical and cerebral ruts you've created over time.

Conjuring up Creativity

I find it comforting to know there's also a scientific basis for coming up with creative ways to break out of old mindsets and build positive new ones.

Robert P. Epstein, Ph.D., former editor-in-chief of *Psychology Today*, invested several decades in studying a concept that pretty much confirmed the old adage, "necessity is the mother of invention."

Epstein's work centered on the now-proven fact that creativity and ingenuity aren't abstract concepts only embodied in an elite few. On the contrary, *everyone* is creative, particularly when they're forced to be.

To prove his point at a workshop in San Diego a few years ago, he invited a volunteer from his audience to come to the front of the room. (Note to self — never, *ever* volunteer when a psychologist is looking for a "victim!")

> *You need chaos in your soul to give birth to a dancing star.*
>
> *~ Nietzsche*

The young woman, all smiles, confidently strode to the front of the group and stood next to an overhead projector.

"Great!" Dr. Epstein said. "Now, I'm going to turn the projector on. You're going to see an image on the screen. You have five minutes to give me a marketing pitch that will make me want to purchase this item."

Still smiling, the woman turned to gaze at the screen, which then revealed an invention that looked like a three-legged stool with a rod protruding from the area that would have been the seat. Her smile dimmed considerably, but she gamely dove in to the challenge.

"What we have here is an auxiliary paper towel or toilet paper dispenser," the woman began strongly, "which can conveniently be taken to any area of your home or office." She whipped out a few more enticing selling points, a reasonable price, and urged listeners to "Call now!" The audience rewarded her with laughter, and she stopped and smiled at Dr. Epstein, apparently awaiting his praise for her good work. "Keep going," he barked.

The woman raised her eyebrows, cleared her throat, paused, and then launched into a detailed pitch about how the device could also help you untangle yarn for knitting projects.

"You're not done," Dr. Epstein challenged her. The people in the audience were starting to empathize with the woman's obvious discomfort. She took a deep breath and launched into yet another spiel, and then another one.

Sweating = Results

Amazingly, as she continued to sweat in front of this large group of strangers and be egged on by the relentless Dr. Epstein, this woman came up with still more creative uses for this bizarre device. By the end of the five minutes, which taskmaster Dr. Epstein extended to about 10 to prove his point, this brave soul had pushed herself beyond reasonable limits to deliver many clever, some absurd and a few brilliant ideas. In fact, some of her best creative solutions bubbled forth long after the initial five minutes and her first few stabs at the challenge were over.

I'm excited by this because it proves a huge part of the BOOM Thinking equation. First, you truly have to experience some discomfort with the way things are before you can reach deep into yourself and find positive, creative ways to make a new mindset. You have to obliterate old limiting ways of thinking, like the woman in Dr. Epstein's demonstration temporarily believing she was completely out of ideas. The same way he was egging on this poor woman and forcing her out of her comfort zone, we need to push ourselves off our apathy and into exciting, inventive, creative new ways of approaching the limiting situations we've allowed in our lives. We each have great reservoirs of creativity just waiting to be tapped.

Exercises.

1. How do your beliefs show up in your body?

2. How do you know when a belief is nourishing you in a positive way?

3. How do you know when a belief is stressing you out and depleting your energy?

4. To stretch your creativity muscles, write down 50 ways you can bring joy into your life or the lives of others.

5. Now that you think you have depleted all of your creative juices, make a list of 50 *more* things that you can do to create joy. I know you can do it! Prove it to yourself.

I Never Metaphor I Didn't Like

Chapter 4

Chapter Four

I Never Metaphor I Didn't Like

From the writings discovered in Mesopotamia, the cradle of civilization, we learn that since ancient times, people have compared one thing to something else to illustrate a point, introduce a new concept, or evoke emotion and imagination. This language of metaphor effectively shifts awareness to a new level and is a powerful tool for teaching and persuasion. It's always been a way for a culture to convey its beliefs and tribal history, and it continues to remain a relevant, empowering tool today.

As we go to press with this book, there's a hysterically funny TV commercial that airs periodically. An attractive, confident-looking woman is in a grocery store, standing in front of the seafood counter. She looks at a large whole fish, and suddenly, a man dressed all in black saunters up behind her. "You're not going to get the entire thing, are you?" he questions. "You wouldn't be able to cook THAT!"

"I'll take the whole salmon, please," the woman tells the clerk, completely ignoring the condescending guy in black. In the next scene, she and Mean Guy in Black are in her kitchen.

"This is just so beyond what you're capable of doing," he mocks her as she sautés, chops, steams and broils a gourmet meal, still ignoring him. "You've REALLY changed," Mean Guy says accusingly before he disappears from her kitchen. In retrospect, you realize Mean Guy is her shadow side, trying to control her through limiting beliefs. At least for this wonderful dinner, she's successfully tuned him out.

Each of us has a shadow side, which is a metaphor for self-doubt, low self-esteem, fear of failure, and all the other negative emotions that can overwhelm and shame us. Just as the commercial personified this aspect of our subconscious mind, I've created an entire personality and alter-ego for my shadow side. Her name is Sasha.

Meet Sasha!

My Sasha is a younger version of Merrill Streep's icy, bitchy, control-freak character in the great movie, *The Devil Wears Prada.* She's excruciatingly thin, impeccably attired and quick to attack my every thought, word and deed with her sharp-tongued insults. She has long, silky, luxurious chestnut hair that she continuously flips back over her shoulder for effect. She's the queen of passive-aggressive snide compliments, such as, "Oh, my dear, that haircut isn't *nearly* as horrid as the last one!" She's my "inner critic," the constant, nagging little voice whispering contemptuous observations like, "You'll never accomplish *that*! What a stupid comment! Just sit down and shut up. No one *cares* what you have to say!"

By channeling all my fears about myself into the metaphor of an inner critic, I'm able to achieve a healthy detachment from the emotional charge of facing uncomfortable things in my real life. I can view my foibles more objectively, and more easily understand and heal them. I know that *I'm* the boss, not Sasha, when I name her, tame her and reframe her — my term for putting boundaries around her and keeping her in check.

> *One day I just said...What if this is just what I look like, and nothing I do changes that? So how much time would I save if I stopped taking that extra second every time I look in the mirror to call myself fat? ...And it turns out I save about ninety-two minutes a week. I can take pottery class.*
>
> ~ Margaret Cho

While Sasha is usually a royal pain in the butt, the *good* thing about having her on my radar is she represents caution and restraint.

Occasionally, having that annoying little voice second-guessing my intentions has resulted in me not making an embarrassing mistake. When I hear that sarcastic, condescending little murmur in the back of my mind, you can bet I stop to BOOM Think her and double-check my internal compass. Is this really right for me? Is this what I should be doing? Is there anything I need to observe or obliterate, or do I need to make a new mindset about a particular issue? If so, I go for it, making a new mindset, tuning out Sasha's biting commentary and continuing on my way with a new level of confidence.

While I have Sasha, other people have the "angel and devil on their shoulder" metaphor playing out in their lives or some similar creation. It's all good as long as we realize this is just a symbolic way of tapping into our subconscious and we take the opportunity to BOOM Think the obstacles our inner critics throw in our paths.

One metaphorical treatment of inner critics created by author Debbie Ford in her book, *The Dark Side of the Light Chasers*, fascinated me. She had an imaginary bus. Various nagging personalities would gradually get on the bus and join the critical voices already clamoring from various rows. Each time the bus stopped, new nagging voices would climb aboard and very few ever stepped off.

While most of the voices spoke up to help out in some roundabout way, like Sasha frequently does, some were just shadowy residue from past hurts, like abusers or teachers who ridiculed and tormented Debbie. Her book explains there are, unfortunately, things that make their way into our psyche that don't have a positive deeper purpose. That's when we have to BOOM Think these metaphoric distractions out of our consciousness and move on, unencumbered by their negativity.

How Metaphors Help Us BOOM Think

Sasha, as dramatic as she is, is just one of the metaphors that color my world. When you're reframing your life and disengaging from your old limiting behaviors and habits, a dramatic metaphor can help you more clearly visualize where you've been and where you want to go. It's an important learning tool and can effortlessly cut across age, gender and social barriers.

Imagine a woman left her hot red sports car unlocked, with the key in the ignition, while she ran into a 7-11 to buy a lottery ticket. Was that a stupid thing for the driver to do? Of course. But is it still illegal if you decide to just hop in the driver's seat, rev up the engine, and take this turbo-powered beauty for a spin? YES, it's illegal, and if you stole the car, you'll be arrested and thrown in jail when you're caught.

This was one of the most powerful and effective metaphors I used

> *As to conforming outwardly and living your own life inwardly, I do not think much of that.*
>
> ~ Henry David Thoreau

when I was working at a rape crisis center. Too often, the victims took on immense guilt and accepted the preposterous idea that somehow the rape was their fault, even when they resisted their attacker, because they were dressed provocatively or they were in the wrong place at the wrong time. Yes, some could have made more prudent choices, but bottom line — just because the vehicle seems accessible doesn't mean it's up for grabs.

Metaphors are Bridges to New Thought Patterns

I've always used metaphors in coaching people, whether I was counseling people about HIV or encouraging entrepreneurs to test the waters with a new product. Because we're such a visual society, vivid metaphors can evoke emotions and quick comprehension in a way that mere instructive statements cannot.

For instance, you're driving down a steep stretch of highway and the car in front of you suddenly swerves off the road. The front of the car smashes through the guardrail and comes to a precarious halt, teetering on the edge of a steep cliff, with an angry ocean churning below. The car's rear tires are coming off the ground as the vehicle rocks back and forth.

What are you going to do? Are you immediately calling 9-1-1 and yelling out to the terrified passengers, telling them to keep still and trying to reassure them from a safe distance? *Or,* do you need to crawl into the smashed-up car and put your own life in imminent danger so you can accurately know what it feels like to be about to fall off a cliff to your death?

That's the dramatic metaphor I've used successfully to illustrate the importance of staying benevolently detached from other people's stuff so you can more effectively help them help themselves.

Frequently when I'm speaking to groups, I'll talk about a metaphoric lighthouse. This towering structure that illuminates a rocky coastline is the perfect symbol to use when I'm talking about being aware of dangers lurking under the surface of a situation. It works on several levels — it talks about shedding light on an issue and simultaneously rising above it. It also serves as a lookout, standing watch for others.

Telling yourself that you're going to evoke the comforting lighthouse metaphor when someone or something pushes your buttons is a powerful way to immediately BOOM potentially negative feelings. For instance, your phone rings, and you see on the caller ID it's your mother-in-law, and the vibes are

> *You've always had the power, my dear. You've had it all along.*
>
> ~ Glinda the Good Witch

not pleasant. Quick! Think, "Lighthouse!" Immediately, you'll see the calming, protective white light beaming out across choppy emotional waters, guiding you safely back to dry land and firm footing. You'll be fine. All is well, metaphorically speaking, of course!

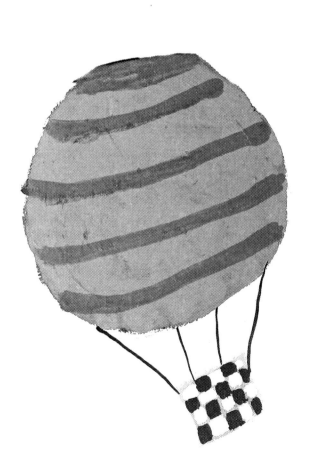

Exercises.

1. What does your "inner critic" bug you about? Why? What buttons can s/he push in your emotional self?

2. Now, pretend this inner critic has a name. What does s/he look like? What does s/he sound like? Let your imagination give him or her life. Invite your inner critic to sit down and have a conversation with you. Even if this exercise stretches your credibility, *go* with it. I promise you you'll get some fascinating insight with this one!

3. Return to the list you created in Chapter One, where I asked you to do a brain dump about limiting beliefs you had in several broad areas. Choose one disempowering situation from each of the sections and write a possible solution. It might make it easier if you imagined that a good friend approached you with that specific problem. How would you encourage her or him to work through it?

4. When you're creating this response, how can you effectively use metaphors to illustrate your points?

What you put out to the world, comes back to you.

"Here's a test to
find out if your
mission in life is
accomplished yet.
If you're alive,
it isn't."

-~ Richard Bach

BOOM Boomerang –
Reality Check Time!

Chapter5

Chapter 5

BOOM Boomerang - Reality Check Time!

I would *dearly* love to tell you that when you've done all your BOOM Thinking processes — you've put on the brakes, observed your current situation, obliterated the self-limiting beliefs and behaviors that were holding you back and then created a positive new mindset — you have successfully moved on and are finished with those old issues forever.

But you've already made it to Chapter Five, and by now you probably realize I'm not going to lie to you. Can't do it! Wouldn't be prudent.

It's taken you months, years and even decades to get ensnared in those old thoughts, words and deeds that wrapped snugly around your ankles and prevented you from taking positive steps forward. As we BOOM Think our way through those issues, we blow up those snares and make some serious progress. We congratulate ourselves for our BOOM achievements and feel well-deserved pride in our courage to release things that no longer serve us.

Then, in the middle of the night on a date that your subconscious circles on your mental calendar, you awaken to realize that *your* Sasha is hissing in your ear, "I'm baaacckkk! Did you *really* think you could obliterate me that easily?"

Ahhhhh, reality. You've just been bopped on the head with a BOOM Boomerang.

Cha-Cha-Changes!

But here's the deal. This is definitely not a failure. When you BOOM Think and set your intention to create a whole new mindset, you've put the change in motion. You've triggered the transformational process that might take a bit longer, but you've already shifted from the place where you were, and that's a good thing. Positive things are starting to happen. They might not be happening as quickly as you would have hoped, but hey, the only thing truly instant in the world is freeze-dried coffee. To get the *real* thing, you have to work from the grounds (sorry, couldn't help myself!) up.

I've mentioned before that change isn't easy, and it's definitely not for sissies. True change isn't just slapping a Pollyanna smile on a situation, either. Repressing how you feel about an issue is like swallowing a time bomb. Sooner or later, my friend, you're going to blow. Admit to yourself that this issue you've tackled isn't immediately "gone," but neither is it destined to permanently derail your best intention to get on the right track. Balance. Perseverance. Patience. Make them your friends.

> *Until we do lose ourselves there is no hope of finding ourselves.*
>
> *~ Henry Miller*

BOOM Thinking is no "Secret"

Let me take a moment to fill you in on the movie *The Secret*. Many viewers consider it a powerful catalyst for helping them focus on what's not working in their lives and envisioning what they desire to manifest instead.

The movie's premise is all about making the connection between our thoughts and feelings, and what we manifest in our lives. In one scene, for instance, a youngster focuses on a red bicycle, even drawing pictures of it, and eventually it shows up on his doorstep. Another scenario involves a huge blue genie repeatedly saying to the man who freed the mythic creature from his golden lamp, "Your wish is my command." Achieving your heart's desire, *The Secret* seems to say, is as simple as commanding the genie to bring your dreams into reality. But here's the rub!

Too many people have come to me after placing their order with the Universe, frustrated and disillusioned that their own equivalent of a shiny red bicycle has yet to be delivered by the "Universal Parcel Service."

I don't feel that *The Secret* is wrong; I just think that the visual of that big blue genie in the sky can throw people. It's too easy to think that all you have to do is sit and wait for your cosmic delivery. In my decades of experience in working with real, live people who have yet to conjure up their own blue magical miracle maker, it's important to emphasize that changing your current situation, or even achieving a sense of peace about an emotionally charged aspect of your life, requires some metaphorical elbow grease on your part.

I would even bet that the lucky few among us who have "instantly" accomplished something, like quitting cigarettes cold turkey, actually attempted to quit many, many times before. Although those efforts didn't completely work back then, they were definitely setting the groundwork to start to move that wheelbarrow out of the old rut and onto a clean, new, smoke-free path.

What I'm saying here is that if something is worth creating a new mindset to achieve and it boomerangs back, just BOOM it again.

Then again. And again, if necessary. Each time you tackle that old issue, it loses some of its emotional charge and some of its power over you.

When the BOOM Boomerang whacks you upside the head, grab that sucker and heave it back into space. Each time, it arcs up a bit higher, takes a bit longer to return to you, and packs significantly less of a punch. Eventually, this issue will have no more bite, and you will have traveled another loop up your evolutionary spiral. Some shifts will take a shorter time than others, but all things you continue to BOOM Think will gradually become less shadowy and more and more transparent.

No matter how big or soft or warm your bed is, you still have to get out of it.

~ Grace Slick

There *Are* No 'Spotless Minds!'

If you happened to catch the awesome Jim Carrey and Kate Winslet movie, *Eternal Sunshine of the Spotless Mind*, you know the sci-fi romantic comedy specifically dealt with the fact that you can't just instantly and completely change your old mindsets. This movie was set in the not-too-distant future, where people who wanted to obliterate any memories of a failed relationship could simply wire up their brain, have the technical folks do a scan to pinpoint exactly where those memories lurked, and zap them away. It was as if the doomed connection had never transpired, so all negative emotional charge to the obliterated relationship simply *expired*. Poof! Kind of a selective lobotomy, if you will.

Until that fictitious process ever becomes reality, barring any kind of amnesia or dementia, we will continue to be steeped in the memories of the people, places and things that have shaped our lives. Depending on how dramatically these experiences affected us, no matter how efficient we are at the BOOM Thinking process — even if we CREATED that process — we're going to have to cut ourselves some slack as we work through all the emotional charge we've assigned to a situation.

I'll be your guinea pig today to dramatically illustrate that very point.

Endless Summer

It was in the summer of 2006 when my husband of 19 years dropped the bombshell — he wanted a divorce. This man and I had been through several lifetimes of change in nearly two decades. We'd changed careers, states, homes, dreams, and our ideas surrounding what being a good parent was all about when both of our wonderful children were diagnosed with multiple learning disabilities. Through all of those challenging stages of our relationship, though, the two of us always faced everything as a team. Together, we worked through one issue after another. Now, suddenly, I had to completely rethink every last detail about literally everything in my life.

I had to break out of all my old mindsets about what it meant to be a single parent, to support myself, to create my own home. My entire life circumstance changed instantly, and every aspect of my world was in flux.

Throughout the transition, I was constantly asking myself, "What are the things I hold to be true at this point in time? Do they really work for me?" When I suddenly became single, up popped this belief that I might not be able to pull it off. I might become destitute, shopping only at Goodwill and living in squalor, eating all my meals from dented cans. I knew I couldn't stay in that state of fear because what you dwell on literally becomes your reality. But let me tell you, the fear wasn't that easy to BOOM away.

The Kroger's Emotional Cave-In

I thought I was handling all the dramatic changes in my world rather well, but actually I was just suppressing everything and telling the world I was FINE. I took a long weekend to visit with my mother in nearby Pigeon Forge, Tennessee, the home of Dollywood. Where better to go to get something off your chest?

> *The real work of life is to allow ourselves to be who we already are, and to have what we already have. The real work is to be passionate, to be holy, be wild, be irreverent, to laugh and cry until you awaken the sleeping spirits, until the ground of your being cleaves and the universe comes flooding in.*
>
> *- Geneen Roth*

Needing to pick up a few groceries, she and I stopped in a Kroger's supermarket. As I was pushing my wobbly-wheeled cart up and down the aisle, my brother in Knoxville called Mom on her cell phone to send his regrets that he wouldn't be able to join us later that day for dinner. I could see she was disappointed, but Mom downplayed her feelings. She told him she understood he couldn't make it, and she was just FINE. (Sound familiar?)

Grabbing the phone from Mom as if possessed by a leathery winged demon of the dark, I lit into my brother with the fury of a class five hurricane. How dare he let her down? What kind of poor excuse for a human being was he? He was a no-good piece of crap, I screamed, hurling insults and spitting vile.

Completely enveloped in my raging wrath, I parked the cart and stomped into the ladies' room to continue my tirade. I screamed, I cried, I put together words that only existed in the seamy underbellies of ships at sea for much longer than humanity could endure. I spewed a vitriolic attack that was punctuated only by toilets quickly flushing and horrified women beating a hasty retreat from this place I had single-handedly turned into the Rest Room from Hell.

There, flanked by sparkling white sinks and accordion pleated paper towels, when I paused for a ragged, tear-filled breath, my flabbergasted brother asked, "Cheri, what the heck is going on here?"

"CHRIS LEFT ME!" I screamed into the cell phone, probably rupturing the poor guy's eardrum. "HE LEFT ME!" I repeated, as if he could have possibly avoided hearing my first bellowing, sobbing pronouncement.

"Cheri, Cheri, let's just stop for a minute," he said in a voice rich with compassion and caring. "I get it, Sweetie. I'm so sorry. Let's calm down a little bit now."

Gradually my sobbing stopped, and I could put on the brakes. Right there in the bathroom at Kroger's, I was able to BOOM Think and realize there had been issues festering for years, but my husband and I hadn't acknowledged them. We truly didn't have a marriage worth saving. Dissolving a romantic relationship we had both outgrown was the smartest thing to do, and it truly was for the best. It was also for the best that I uncorked all the sad feelings I'd been frantically stuffing into a closet for years. Pus always comes out with a splinter; my wonderful brother reminded me when my repressed emotions erupted that day in a head-spinning rant that probably made that poor bathroom require repainting. I am definitely too embarrassed to ever go back in that store!

The "Kroger's Emotional Cave-in" became the turning point in creating a healthy new mindset about the divorce. After reaching that low point, I was more than ready to obliterate that state of mind and create a new place in the world for me to share my work, raise my kids, and get on with my life in a positive way.

Reconnecting the Dots

I immediately began to do what I teach others to do. I stopped and had a long, hard look at my life. Let me tell you, it was tough. I evaluated my strengths and vulnerabilities. I observed my emotions and behaviors. I consciously decided the shadowy, panicky feelings had to *go*, and I had to shift my temporary belief that my life was going to be all about scarcity and desperation.

Even with passionate, constant BOOM Thinking on my part, it was tough going. I took each minute, hour and day one step at a time, recreating a safe and secure space for the kids and me. Any time Sasha would grab me by the throat and scream, "You are TOAST!"

— I'd take a deep breath and mentally shove her into the microwave. Instead of being seduced by the idea of just giving up, I'd take a deep breath, BOOM Think through another emotional speed bump, and keep going.

I found a sweet, comfortable craftsman style home in a vibrant neighborhood within walking distance of parks, restaurants and shops. I discovered I had enough money to buy beautiful, chic furniture and decorations that perfectly suited my new home's charming personality, and mine, too. My coaching and speaking business ironically just took off — more proof of the old adage that you best teach what you most need to learn! True friends rallied round, and new ones appeared to add another rich dimension to my life. I was starting to see the light at the end of the tunnel.

So much of making BOOM Thinking work — and making your life work, too — boils down to knowing that you have options. You get to choose which things will reduce you to a ranting maniac in a grocery store bathroom and which things you will deflect to maintain your emotional stability. What meaning will you give to the things unfolding in your life? Which things will hold your attention? Which things will you release? While BOOM Thinking is an organic, constantly changing process, and every once in a while you'll encounter a BOOM boomerang, you still get to chart your life course and drive the car.

The Two Wolves

You know me and my metaphors. Please let me share an ancient Native American one.

An old Grandfather said to his grandson, who came to him with anger at a friend who had done him an injustice, "Let me tell you a story. I too, at times, have felt great hate for those who have taken so much, with no sorrow for what they do. But hate wears you down and does not hurt your enemy. It's like taking poison and wishing your enemy would die."

"I have struggled with these feelings many times."

"It is as if there are two wolves inside me; one is good and does no harm. He lives in harmony with all around him and does not take offense when no offense was intended. He will only fight when it is right to do so, and in the right way."

"But the other wolf... ah! The littlest thing will send him into a fit of temper. He fights everyone, all of the time, for no reason. He cannot

think because his anger and hate are so great."

"It is helpless anger, for his anger will change nothing. Sometimes it is hard to live with these two wolves inside me, for both of them try to dominate my spirit."

The boy looked intently into his Grandfather's eyes and asked, "Which one wins, Grandfather?"

The Grandfather smiled and quietly said, "The one I feed."

Which wolf are *you* choosing to feed?

> *It took me a long time not to judge myself through someone else's eyes.*
>
> *~ Sally Field*

Limiting Words

Besides choosing which wolf you're going to feed, it's important to choose words that will empower you and help you shift your way of being in the world. Our subconscious mind is listening intently to the words we speak, and it takes them all quite literally. For instance, if you're always saying, "I know I'm not going to get my work done today," guess what? You've just effectively programmed yourself to come up short — and you definitely will.

It's the same with saying limiting words like, "I have just enough money to squeak by." Guess who'll be squeaking all the way to the pawn shop?

As you start to BOOM Think through the beliefs and habits that have limited you in the past, it's time to BOOM the old language that kept your feet to the fire, too. Here's a handy chart to help you speak in the language of positive, powerful change, and **deflect a bunch of BOOM Boomerangs in the process.**

Instead of saying….	Try saying….
"I'll never finish this project!"	"I'll continue to work on this a set amount of time every day until it's completed."
"I always date losers!"	"I'm ready to find a special someone who would make an excellent spouse for a long and happy marriage."
"I can't"	"I choose not to."
"I hope," "I might," "I want to," or "I wish I could"	"I will!"
"I'll never be (thin), (beautiful), (rich)…"	"I am BOOM Thinking to create positive new options in my life."
"I could never do that!"	"I am starting today to accomplish that."
"I need…"	"I am creating…"
"I couldn't accept that!"	"Thank you!"

Exercises

1. What's something you've said in the last week that's diminished your power?

2. Write down a positive, proactive alternative response you will use in a similar situation.

3. What's an issue you've BOOMED that's shown up again in your life?

4. How will you fine-tune your BOOM Thinking process to send this BOOM Boomerang back out of your life?

"There are
no gains
without pain."

-- Benjamin
Franklin

I Haven't Got Time
for the Pain

(Wrong!)

 Chapter 6

Chapter 6

I Haven't Got Time for the Pain (Wrong!)

I can't visualize a life that's totally blissful with everyone thinking only happy thoughts all the time. We don't learn from that. There are some people out there who will tell you that's not true, but they're either highly enlightened (rock on!) or totally delusional. YES, I consider myself optimistic, but I'm also realistic. I firmly believe clouds *and* silver linings coexist in everyone's life, and our lives are all the richer because of it.

To me, the goal at the end of a lifetime or a day or an hour is that the good outweighs the bad. If you don't have *some* pain, you won't appreciate, recognize or work toward achieving the good times.

Robert Bly's *A Little Book on the Human Shadow* beautifully illustrates this delicate dance of balance in our lives. He says the brighter the sun, the darker the shadow. There's no escaping the fact that there definitely is a direct relationship between the two. For instance, when you look outside on a cloudy day, there's very little shadow. It all looks pretty flat and neutral, and everything seems to kind of run together. In contrast, on a bright day when the sun is bathing the landscape in brilliant splashes of golden light, the shadow of a tall tree will be equally as dark. Dark doesn't have to mean suffering. It doesn't have to be an overwhelming negative. It just *is*. If you want a life that's like a neutral cloudy day all the time, you'll never feel great pain or sorrow, but you'll also never get to feel exhilarating, heart-warming joy, either.

A cartoon I loved had a huge, menacing dragon spewing flames, and a tiny knight tilting his helmeted head back to stare up into the glowering eyes of his green, scaly foe. The caption read, "No guts, no glory!" The greater the risk, the more you stand to gain or lose.

Finding Your Rhythms

BOOM Thinking is all about getting in tune with the rhythms of your life and going after the good stuff you want to bring into your sphere of influence. It's about honestly evaluating your current circumstances and determining the level of predictability, or comfort, you deem desirable. You might decide, "I only want my life to vary this much in intensity," or "I *love* this intensity and uncertainty! More risk! Bring it on!" A friend I respect deeply admits he makes decisions based on keeping himself safe from pain. He's also aware that those same decisions limit the amount of joy in his life. He's made that conscious choice, and he says it works for him.

In evaluating how your life is working for you on all levels, there are going to be people who suffer more discomfort from their current mindsets than others. Honestly, some people will decide to forego the "glory" goals and opt instead for a seemingly predictable, safe, risk and pain-free circumstance.

> *Success has more to do with the learner you are than with the expert you have become. Success thrives on the compost of your errors.*
>
> *~ Molly Gordon*

A generation or two ago, this really was the norm. You got a company job right out of high school or college, and that's where you stayed. You were loyal to that company, and in turn, the company took care of you, too. You'd get health benefits, occasional promotions and raises, and, after 40 or so years, you'd get a nice retirement party, a gold watch, and an adequate pension. Taking that first and only job was like stepping inside a snug cocoon, where you could always feel safe and secure.

Well, dragon slayers, times certainly have changed, haven't they? Now, the norm is to not only switch companies several times in your career, but to also switch careers a time or two, at least. Many of those companies our parents and grandparents swore allegiance to are now defunct. They've outsourced jobs to foreign countries or they've slashed benefits and pensions. There *is* no safe, secure cocoon any more. That's why this is such a great time to figure out what it is that makes you tick — to find those things you just can't help but do that you listed back in Chapter Two — and just *go* for them.

This is not the time to "settle" and sentence yourself to existing in that velvet rut because even though it's sucking away your vital life force, at least it's familiar. This is the time to acknowledge the pain, BOOM your butt out of that rut, and start living on all cylinders.

Life-changing Milestones

There are some significant transitions in our society specifically designed to shake up things in your world. These are the milestones when you begin to change how you see yourself and redefine your role:

- You were a student, and now you've graduated to "the real world."

- You were single, and now you're married.

- You were childless, and now you're a parent.

- You were hourly, and now you're a salaried manager.

- You were married, and now you're divorced or widowed.

- You were in your 30s, and now you're in your 40s. Or 60s. Or beyond.

Even though these shifts are a natural part of life, we've already acknowledged that change is usually gritty, scary and frequently painful, and changing your thoughts and beliefs is work. In our society, we tend to have a cultural craving for that silver bullet, that instant karma that will provide all the answers, oversimplify the situation, fix our pain and protect us from any discomfort.

That truly is a very Western view. Traditionally, in Western medicine when you have physical, mental or emotional pain, you high-tail it to the nearest M.D. and get pills to fix it. Former US Surgeon General Dr. Jocelyn Elders was booted out of that prestigious post a mere 15 months after being sworn in because she emphatically criticized that "wait until it's broken" methodology. "The US has a 'sick care' system, not a 'health care' system," she insisted. Conversely, Eastern philosophy says — and I'm paraphrasing here, all you literal people! — "Come to us *before* you're ill, and we'll consciously come up with ways to keep you healthy."

If we approach our lives in the typical Western way, we keep running around in frantic, blood-pressure boosting circles. We lose yet another job, we break up with the tenth boyfriend in a year, and we put on those 20 pounds we'd just lost before we finally think, "Hummmm. I'm not happy with my life. Something needs to change."

East Meets West

What I'm proposing with BOOM Thinking is a much more Eastern approach. Constantly put on the brakes and take inventory. What are my thoughts and beliefs? What's crucially important to me right now? Is that really what I want to be thinking? If what you're dwelling on and experiencing is *not* in alignment with your core values, change it. Now.

> Only one thing is more frightening than speaking your truth. And that is not speaking.
>
> - Naomi Wolfe

Regardless of how you get to a new mindset — through pain or through mindful choice — I think you have to do a list of pros and cons, a risks and benefits assessment beforehand.

For example, let's say you are going to change your beliefs about your eating habits. You're going to start making different choices about the foods you consume, and the benefits are many. You're going to feel better. You're going to sleep better. You're going to lower your triglycerides, your weight, your cholesterol, your blood pressure. You'll achieve all of those positive results if you stick to your new plan.

However, it's important to look at other potential results, too. When you shed some poundage, you're probably going to be getting more attention from people who are now attracted to you. How do you keep from feeling emotionally and physically vulnerable in your slimmer new body?

Serving up Guilt

Another potential hot spot, and this is a *big* one, is that you're going to have to disappoint your family when you go to your grandmother's house and say, "No, thank you! This time I won't be eating any of that incredible pecan pie you baked just for me!" One of my grandmother's limiting beliefs is that if you don't eat her food, you don't love her. And now, you're going to have to figure out how to deal with your whole family, who's been telling you they love you by feeding you. When you tell them no, you don't want to eat their food because you're making new lifestyle choices, you're tapping into a whole new dynamic. You're also going to trigger family members into saying, "What? So now you think you're better than us? Our food's not *good* enough for you? Our family's always been fat; you're *never* going to be thin!"

What if your spouse is fat and has loved gobbling down your rich, buttery, creamy, and deep-fried cooking? If you suddenly decide to switch to fruits and veggies, there's a fat chance *that* won't cause a ruckus at home!

I'm being completely honest with you here. The risks and potential pain of making positive changes can be enormous. Of course, the payoffs are transformational, but you must be prepared to fight the good fight while you're BOOM Thinking your way toward this new and improved way of living your life.

In my experience, this "tirade of truth" is critical in helping to get you through the treacherous waters lurking between your current state of being and your safe harbor.

I use this type of gritty confrontational reality a lot when I'm talking about sexuality or drugs. Is it safer to wear a condom? What are the downsides to using a condom? It doesn't feel as good. It's more awkward. You have to have it with you. You might have to have a conversation about using it. You might have to touch yourself while someone's watching you. And so on and so on. Who wants to go through all of that? No one! But when you weigh the inconvenience of using a condom versus the very real possibilities of pregnancy, sexually transmitted diseases, or even HIV, people — even young ones with crazed hormones — can frequently understand.

Instead of just glossing over the truth and saying, "Oh, it's going to be great," I acknowledge that, for a while, whether we're talking about HIV/AIDS prevention or switching careers, you're going to be uncomfortable. The velvet rut you were entrenched in felt so familiar. You weren't happy, but you were getting by — and it did serve you.

> *The only way to live is to accept each minute as an unrepeatable miracle, which is exactly what it is: a miracle and unrepeatable.*
>
> ~ Storm Jameson

BOOM Thinking through History

While I've given this process a spiffy new name, it's actually an ancient concept that's been shaking up history for millennia. Just about every religion has its roots in a BOOM Thinking model of an enlightened individual — Moses, Jesus, Buddha, Mohammad, and all the rest — putting on the brakes, observing what's happening, obliterating the old way of being, and creating a whole new spiritual mindset that gets adopted by the masses.

In the more secular world, you can bet that Susan B. Anthony had to BOOM her old way of being in the 19th century before she became a high-profile political activist for the anti-slavery and temperance movements, and, of course, an activist for woman's right to vote.

In the contemporary arena, besides Oprah, whom I saluted in Chapter Two, I have the deepest respect for the way Christopher Reeve and Michael J. Fox shifted their mindsets when they were presented with cataclysmic health challenges. I would bet that Christopher never spent a minute thinking about being a quadriplegic until he suddenly became one. He completely redefined what it meant to have "super powers." Through their inner strength and grace, both men adapted their mindsets to become powerful advocates, helping untold numbers of people by raising awareness and hopes for a cure.

Sandra Day O'Conner wasn't held back by the fact that no woman had ever served on the highest court in the land. She made history and some giant leaps for womankind as the first female Supreme Court Justice. Sally Ride, America's first female astronaut, also created a new mindset for women and launched a new era of equal opportunities in space.

Jane Fonda and the Dixie Chicks made history by shifting old mindsets about politics and US involvement in foreign wars. They were all castigated for their initial outspokenness, but eventually, public opinion radically shifted, and their new mindset was embraced by many.

Every time a BOOM Thinker builds a new mindset, an angel gets its wings. Or at least that person's spirit gets wings, and it flies up to a place of higher consciousness to ponder, "If I could successfully BOOM this particular situation, what else in my life, or in the world, can I transform?"

I've listed some truly headline-worthy precedents, but powerful examples of what BOOM Thinking can accomplish really begin much closer to home. Not that I'm old, thank you — I've spent quality time BOOM Thinking THAT limiting belief! — but when I was in high school, the Key Club was still primarily a male-dominated domain. I refused to give up my power, though, and eventually became a Key Club Lt. Governor for the Knoxville, Tennessee region.

> *The trick is not how much pain you feel – but how much joy you feel. Any idiot can feel pain. Life is full of excuses to feel pain, excuses not to live, excuses, excuses, excuses.*
>
> *~ Erica Jong*

A neighbor grew up in a family of smokers. After trying to quit several times through the decades, she finally got serious. She put on the brakes, observed the health issues plaguing other family members, rejected the idea that she was hopelessly addicted to cigarettes, and convinced herself that she WOULD stop smoking. Now, years later, she's still smoke-free and breathing easy. Yes, it was a difficult habit to break, but it couldn't survive the scrutiny and focus of her BOOM Thinking.

When my dear grandmother was suddenly widowed after decades of marriage, this woman, who had always been supported by her husband, paused to consider her situation, then decided to completely buck tradition and find a job. Despite the skeptics who clucked their disapproval, Mammy found work she loved. Besides creating a comfortable financial situation for herself, Mammy widened her circle of friends and enriched her life on many levels.

BOOM Thinking Your "Mistakes"

It's so cool to realize that things appearing to be a problem can, with some focused BOOM Thinking, turn out to be, as Martha Stewart would say, a very good thing.

Do you know how the Ivory Soap catchphrase, "So pure it floats," came to be? One of the workers at a soap factory left a batch in the mixer too long and whipped too much air into the ingredients. Instead of sinking to the bottom of a tub, this lighter bar bobbed to the surface and stayed there. While management's first inclination was to toss the botched batch, a BOOM Thinker at the company realized an opportunity to create a new mindset and advertised "floating soap" as preferable to the traditional heavier sinking kind. Millions of bars and profitable dollars later, Ivory Soap still rises to the top.

Making New Mindsets About Money

Technically, this section doesn't *have* to be in the "Pain" chapter, but the majority of us probably still equate a lackluster bank account with painful circumstances. Thankfully, our society is shifting mindsets about that with some powerful results.

The 80s and 90s were all about accumulating stuff and the money to acquire it. In 1988, *Wall Street* won picture of the year, and Machiavellian financial leader Gordon Gekko's pronouncement that "Greed is good!" leaped from the big screen to people's lips everywhere.

In the shadow of Enron's demise, the burst real estate bubble, and the wildly fluctuating economy, people are earnestly creating new mindsets about the importance and power of money. Somehow, that mini-mansion and summers in Tuscany pale in comparison to good health, quality time with the family, and making cost-efficient consumer choices that respect the environment and sustainability.

Sometimes it has to be a stress-induced medical crisis that causes people to BOOM Think their life choices and jump off the fast track. Occasionally, parents stop to really look at their kids and realize they have no idea who these not-quite-grown-up people are. The best instances are when people realize they haven't followed their true passion, and a juicy paycheck is no substitute for deep inner joy and a sense of purpose.

I read and walked for miles at night along the beach... searching endlessly for someone wonderful who would step out of the darkness and change my life. It never crossed my mind that that person could be me

~ Anna Quindlen

BOOM Thinking is a great process to help people redefine what "prosperity" really is and reset their life path in a direction that will bring them happiness and peace.

More people are rethinking what it means to be whole, discovering that no matter how many assets they have, something's missing until they listen to their heart and honor that longing.

Creating a new mindset about what actually constitutes wealth in your life might pinch a bit at first. If you're dealing with a vague sense that something's off, though, BOOM Thinking might be your only way to reconnect to your true self and your joy.

Exercises

1. In your BOOM journal, list the things you wanted to be when you were a child. Don't edit or analyze! If your 7-year-old self wanted to be a "Dragon Slayer" or a "Cake Decorator," write it down!

   This exercise is important because children are more in touch with their heart's desires. They haven't yet encountered roadblocks in life that separate them from their dreams. You can frequently get back in touch with old passions by looking at your life through a child's eyes.

2. Review your list. How many of the things have you abandoned? Why? Don't just go for the superficial answer, like, "Well, there ARE no dragons to slay!" On a deeper and metaphorical level, you'll realize there really *are* dragons in our world. They just might be festooned in power suits instead of green scales.

   For any of the items on that list that still elicit a flicker of interest, do some BOOM Thinking to see what new mindsets you can create to embrace those childhood passions and bring them into your life now.

"Above all, be the heroine of your life, not the victim."

-- Nora Ephron

My Life in BOOM-Speak

Chapter 7

Chapter 7

My Life in BOOM-Speak

After every event, each speaking engagement and all my workshops, women come up to me and say, "Cheri, we love listening to you because you're just so *real*!" They like that I always do a lot of self-disclosure — not from an academic place, but from my heart. Sometimes I'll hear myself revealing *very* personal information, and Sasha will hiss, "What are you *doing*?? You can't tell them that! Why would they ever listen to someone who's done something *that* stupid?"

That's when I just have to swallow hard, mentally slap a strip of duct tape across Sasha's crimson-stained mouth, and continue sharing.

As I air those gritty, gutsy moments in my life when I've blasted out of the latest corner I painted myself into, grabbed a wild new opportunity by the tail and hung on for dear life, I can see people in the audience *get* it. We share a moment; we understand we're all in this together. That's why I can authentically stand in front of you and say, "HELL yes, this BOOM Thinking stuff works! I've survived, I've thrived, and you can do this too!"

I'm a case study in how powerfully BOOM Thinking can propel us forward through soul-wrenching obstacles — even though I didn't have a name for the process until a few decades after I began using it.

Southern Roots

I grew up the only daughter in a devout Southern Baptist family. My parents absolutely did the best they could with what they knew at the time, and I remember my father frequently saying to me, "Cheri, all I ask of you is that you always do your best." I walked a straight and narrow path, went to church religiously, and never really thought about any other options.

My life took a dramatic left turn on a sunny Saturday afternoon during my senior year in high school. My mother, a friend and I were preparing a church in a rough part of town for a wedding. When a man dressed as a custodian entered the banquet hall as my friend and I were arranging flowers, we just assumed he should be there. Before we realized something was wrong, the man struck me in the back of the head and started to force us into the kitchen. About then, my mother, who was handling the catering, entered the fellowship hall. The man immediately pushed my friend and me into the kitchen, told us he'd kill my mom if we made any noise, then grabbed my mother and dragged her into a church bathroom, where he raped her. He then fled the scene.

We were all traumatized. How could this happen in a church, where you're supposed to be safe?

Being such faithful church members, we expected our ministers and deacons to offer solace, counseling and support. To our amazement, we were ignored. It was as if somehow *we* were to blame for the devastating attacks. Decades later, one of the deacons involved admitted they had all let us down, and they should have been there to help us heal on physical, mental, emotional and spiritual levels. At the time, though, we were completely abandoned by everyone.

There Are ALWAYS Options

Even though I was only a teenager, I realized I had two options. I could give up, accept all the misplaced blame, and live my life in shadow and humiliation. Or I could get angry — at the attacker, at the pastoral team that wasn't there for us, at our community that whispered behind our backs that we shouldn't have been in that part of town in the first place. Let me tell you, I got angry.

I emphatically corrected the whisperers, pointing out that we were in a *church* on a Saturday *afternoon*. We were not being provocative; we were preparing this sacred space for a wedding. And to top it off, we had been completely abandoned by the clergy that should have supported us.

Anger can be a wonderful force for blasting through old mindsets. That life-changing experience in a little southern church absolutely made me put on the brakes, observe what was happening on many levels, obliterate my old idea that I had no say and no options, and led me to create a powerful new framework for my life. I was not a voiceless victim. I was a force for good. I would use my own painful experience to help others understand sexuality issues, particularly those involving force.

> *We're constantly being told what other people think we are, and that's why it is so important to know yourself.*
>
> *~ Sarah McLachlan*

I volunteered as a rape crisis counselor in college. I got married, earned a master's degree in health education and got a job with the Health Department in Charlotte, North Carolina, concentrating on HIV counseling and testing. I also worked with Planned Parenthood, educating and training professionals across the state. I taught social workers and teachers how to talk to young people about sex. I also helped parents understand how to discuss sex with their kids. I taught people how to protect themselves and have positive views about their own sexuality. I was challenging people to take responsibility for their lives, to realize they had options, to claim their power and passion, and to give their life purpose.

As I was reaching my stride in inspiring and motivating others, I was starting to rethink my long-term opportunities in staying with non-profit organizations. I gave up my counseling positions when my husband and I moved to Asheville in the heart of the Smoky Mountains in western North Carolina.

My BOOM Thinking Timeline

If you've been to one of my presentations, you already know how I love to share intimate details with my audience. While I call it "being authentic," my artist friend Moni Hill calls it "living without filters."

With that in mind, I'm condensing major milestones in my life into BOOM moments:

1994

Limiting Old Belief: Sawyer is born; can I move from being a working person to being a full-time stay-at-home mom? It was as if I woke up one day and I was in an alien world where Birkenstock-sporting women made their own organic baby food, scorned disposable diapers, and taught their infants French and physics. How did *this* happen? The next few years were an "environmentally correct" patchouli haze as I struggled to find my footing and reframe my life.

BOOM Solution: I immersed myself in the full-time mom role, making my own baby food (but still using disposable diapers!). I created a vibrant stay-at-home mom community and still keep in touch with some of the treasured friends I met.

Around 1996

Limiting Old Belief: I don't want to be a full-time stay-at-home mom anymore; can I revive my career? I was becoming an "accidental entrepreneur." Different groups hired me to come speak; various companies contracted with me to present workshops. Instead of having a clearly thought-out business plan, I was hopping from project to project, secure in the knowledge that my husband was bringing home the steady paychecks.

BOOM Solution: I didn't get another "job," but I started actively marketing myself as a consultant and trainer. I developed a weekend retreat called "Renewal" for the stressed-out professional, which was a huge success but a financial failure.

1997

Limiting Old Belief: Can I go from being hired as a consultant to successfully creating and running my own business?

BOOM Solution: I just started applying for contracts to see if I could get any, and it worked. I began putting together my own company.

1998-99

Limiting Old Belief: There's something missing in my life!

BOOM solution: I hire "Comfort Queen" Jennifer Louden as my first coach and discover that besides counseling people and conducting trainings, I want to speak to audiences. So I do, and immediately start booking presentations.

2002-2003

Limiting Old Belief: Could I continue my HIV and sexuality consulting work and also be a business coach? How do I reconcile the three very different areas of my work — coaching, speaking and counseling?

BOOM Solution: I hire Isabel Parlett to help me reconcile all my interests, and out of that comes the BOOM Thinking model. I give a name to the process I'd been using my entire life.

2004-on

From this point on, I actively use BOOM Thinking to process just about every aspect of my life.

I started identifying myself as a professional. I sought out supportive groups that mirrored my own values and life situation — a dynamic church and women business owners focused on growing their professional skills, profits, and network of contacts. I was among people I identified with and respected. I reconnected with myself. I was back! This was also about the time I began putting a specific name — BOOM Thinking — to the process that had been an important part of my life since my pivotal experience in that little southern church.

Passion = Purpose

You might ask at this point, "How much of BOOM thinking is about following your passion?" I would have to say, a *lot*. You can look at it as being a pain reliever or a divining rod. Breaking out of old mindsets is, at the very *least*, a way to release hurtful old judgments. You have an expectation that's not in alignment with who you are, or it's somehow not what you want. Releasing that expectation relieves the pressure.

In my personal experience, though, it's much more than that. When you go deeper into understanding why you adopted that old mindset in the first place, frequently, you can reconnect with your passion. It's so far beyond just "scratching an itch;" it's fixing that hole in your heart where your peace and joy drained out. You start living again on all cylinders. After experiencing a deep hurt, you have a unique opportunity to focus your energy on healing that part of yourself and actually making it one of your most enduring strengths.

I've already shared my "Kroger's Emotional Cave-in" adventure in Chapter Five, so you know how using BOOM Thinking helped me navigate my divorce. It was an emotionally draining life passage, but I think I'm healthier now. There was a lot of discomfort in my marriage for years, but not enough to motivate me to make a shift. Unlike my friend who's content to live his life in "neutral," I'm a passionate, sensitive, sensuous soul who wants to squeeze every ounce of gusto from each and every minute of life. To me, one of the saddest things in a marriage is mediocrity. Divorce hurts, but it also gives you the opportunity to fill a wounded heart with real passion and love somewhere down the road.

It's important to me that you know that BOOM Thinking isn't just some cool-sounding theory I dreamed up while sipping sweet tea on a big front porch on a lazy summer afternoon. This process of honestly owning and analyzing what's not going great in my life, releasing it, and shifting into a whole new positive direction is at the core of my very being. I have lived the truth of its effectiveness, over and over. I continue to call upon it to help me find focus, direction and peace of mind.

I offer it to you in the sincere hope it brings you similar balance and joy.

> *There are only two things that prevent you from accomplishing your goals -- fear and self doubt. When you learn to trust yourself and ask for help, the world gets a whole lot easier.*
>
> *~ Wyatt Webb*

Now, in the next chapter, we'll stop talking about *me* and refocus on you!

Exercises.

1. In your BOOM journal, create your own timeline. Look back at the times you were at a crossroads or were faced with special challenges. What beliefs did you hold when you chose a particular path? Would you make the same decisions today?

2. If you see several similar situations cropping up repeatedly, what belief do you hold that keeps you making the same limiting choices? What belief do you need to build to allow you to make different, positive choices that will move you forward?

3. Now look to the future. What crossroads are you likely to encounter that may require you to examine your beliefs and make new mindsets? Some possibilities include an empty nest, retiring, health issues, caring for elderly parents or downsizing your home.

"And the day
came when the risk
to remain tight in
a bud was more
painful than the risk
it took to blossom."

~ Anais Nin

How Dare You NOT
Be a BOOM Thinker?!

Chapter 8

Chapter 8

How Dare You NOT
Be a BOOM Thinker?!

Mary Elizabeth Kingston, a talented architect, did a coaching class with me and laid out a detailed plan for her company. A year later, she sent me a note to update me on her progress. She'd accomplished all her key goals. She and her husband bought a home within walking distance of work, so they were driving much less. She'd shifted to more environmentally friendly architectural projects, and she enjoyed more quality time with her daughter. She thought she was trying to fix her business (kingston-architecture. com) but discovered she was actually trying to create a life that more accurately reflected her personal values. Now, she has both.

Robin Payne attended my workshop for women entrepreneurs while

> *The world is not happening to us. We are happening to it. We are molding it, shaping it, creating the good and bad with our thoughts.*
>
> ~ Iyanla Vanzant

she was pregnant. Despite the fact that her life was already about to drastically change, Robin identified several limiting beliefs, put them to the side, and "gave birth" to a new business dedicated to organic infant products (thegreenrobin.com) and to her baby at the same time. "When I look out into the world of people who are stuck in the fear of 'I can't do it' and trudge to the same unrewarding job every day," Robin wrote, "I am thankful that I continually go out on a limb. That's where all the good fruit is!"

Another woman attended one of my retreats, did some deep BOOM Thinking about her life, and gradually lost 75 pounds over the next year.

Getting Un-Stuck

In my work to help people BOOM Think their way to a positive new place in their life, I've noticed that nearly everyone says, "I feel stuck." Often, there's a sense of a lack of momentum, or some unidentified thing that's holding them back. They may initially say it's about money, but even there, you can dissect it into lots of different subsets.

For people who are first sticking a toe into the BOOM Think tank, it's important to take a general inventory and ask a few questions. Sometimes you have to stir that historical pot just a bit to see what comes to the top.

- What were the mindsets in the home where you grew up?

- What were the different mindsets you had during certain ages of your life?

- What were the mindsets you heard from your church, temple or place of worship?

- When did you realize you had a mindset different from that of your family?

More often than not, the beliefs that are really holding us back aren't the obvious ones. For instance, Mary Elizabeth, the architect, thought she was creating a new mindset for her business, but she was actually addressing the lifestyle values she craved for her family and herself.

Look Deep Within

Because so many of our limiting beliefs have deep roots, when people are working to identify them I encourage them to go a few steps deeper than what they might initially think is the roadblock.

It's regular people stepping outside of their comfort zone and leaving the limiting yet familiar confines of their velvet rut who accomplish exceptional things. A rut is not typically where you experience a joyful, juicy, exuberant life.

Let's be clear that when I say "exceptional things," that's purely a relative term. If you think you have to clean your bathroom every day but you know your time is better spent playing with your children, the day you don't clean your bathroom to play Chutes and Ladders™ with the kids definitely qualifies as an exceptional day.

We're all in a rut to some degree. When we get uncomfortable enough, and usually *only* then, we become truly willing and able to finally identify old limiting beliefs and release them. It bears repeating that significant change will not be a euphoric thing with doves carrying banners saying, "AWESOME job!" and angel choirs singing your praises. Instead, you're probably going to think, "This is hard. I want to go back to the way it was." Nothing worth having comes easy. It's true. But keep your eyes on the prize.

Where do you want to end up? What are the long range goals for which you're creating these new mindsets? Visualize them in your mind's eye. Inhale the great emotional satisfaction of having already achieved them. Tune in to how you feel now that you're holding this victory in your hand. You've heard the rallying cry, "What you believe, you achieve." You know what? That's true.

Who are you to shift old limiting beliefs and become incredibly successful? I'll turn that right around and give you the challenge I fling at my audiences and clients. Who are you NOT to be a BOOM Thinker?

'Predictable' Does NOT Mean 'Safe'

Being an entrepreneur or a risk taker does seem to tempt fate. For instance, if someone wants to be a songwriter and decides to quit a corporate executive post to pursue that dream, they're giving up a steady paycheck, health benefits, and to a great degree, their credibility — at least until they have a big hit. Or another example — my assistant Stefanie's grandmother went back to school to pursue her Ph.D. after she divorced and was raising four young children by herself. Who the heck does something like *that*?

Wouldn't it just be easier to have a normal job? Superficially, yes — but...no. When your work or your life isn't in alignment with your passion, ultimately, you're going down the wrong track, and you're going to get derailed.

It's important to understand that as you put the BOOM process to work in your life, the community around you can make or break you, and it can interfere with your best efforts to BOOM Think. You first determine who's not working in your circle. You learn how to identify what Julia Cameron, author of *The Artist's Way*, calls "crazy makers" — those people who just have the innate ability to create drama and discord, knocking you and everyone else around them off balance. How do you empower the people around you? Who is leeching away your energy and sucking you dry in the process? After you've identified them, how do you shift them to a place where you're not handing them your power?

Women are particularly susceptible to this. We're taught to keep the peace, make everything nice and tidy, and keep everyone happy. Well, news flash! That is a phenomenally deep and potentially destructive self-limiting belief. As Ben Franklin said, **"The Constitution only gives people the right to pursue happiness. You have to catch it yourself."**

Is It Time For A Coach?

Frequently, a quick and effective way to move toward your goal of BOOM Thinking your personal and professional life is to hire a coach. This can be a strategically essential part of your success if you're not confident about your level of self-insight, your ability to be accurately introspective, and the strength and health of your current community. In my model of the world, if those things are questionable, then a coach is paramount. How do you find one? These days, "coach" is such a generic word for a lot of things. I think it's important to determine if you need a coach or a therapist. For some of the issues that come up around limiting beliefs, therapy is important. Much of therapy focuses on why you have certain thoughts and how you move beyond them. Meanwhile, coaching deals with "so what?" and "NOW what?"

One question I love to pose to coaching clients goes very deep, and usually provides a clue about the mindset you'd most like to shift: "What's the one thing that, if it were gotten rid of, would provide the greatest satisfaction and allow you to move forward the most?"

A coach comes in when you've identified what you want to shift, specifically to help you shift it. Be wary of the coach who tries to handle a client's deep emotional pain; that job should be reserved for a therapist. That doesn't mean good coaching can't *feel* therapeutic. But if a coach starts to sound as if they do therapy, watch out!

> *When I stand before God at the end of my life, I would hope that I would not have a single bit of talent left, and could say, "I used everything you gave me."*
>
> -Erma Bombeck

If you're serious about making major positive, permanent shifts in your life, you also don't want a business consultant who just tells you what to do. Those three terms — therapist, coach and consultant — are misused and thrown around a lot. Talk to your friends and see how they can help you figure out what direction you want to go before you pay money to a coach you don't know, and who may or may not be qualified.

Exercises.

In your BOOM journal, write down your thoughts about the following questions:

1. What were the mindsets in the home where you grew up?

2. What were the mindsets you had during certain ages of your life?

3. What were the mindsets you heard from your church, temple or place of worship?

4. If you had a mindset different from that of your family, when did you discover that fact? What did that mean for you?

5. What is draining your energy? What causes stress or distracts you from focusing on your goals?

6. Where do you want to end up? How do you want to "be" in the process of getting there — frenetic and crazy or peaceful and calm?

7. What's the one thing that, if it were gotten rid of, would provide the greatest satisfaction and allow you to move forward the most?

8. What are ways you can bring your vision into your everyday life? For instance, mind mapping, vision boards, collages, a Buddha statuette on a desk, or a framed picture of Italy where you can see it daily.

"When you pray, move your feet."

~ Quaker Proverb

BOOM Thinking In Action

Chapter 9

BOOM THINKING IN ACTION

I can honestly say that to me, sharing the concept of BOOM Thinking is more of a "mission" than a job. That's why I'm personally very moved and excited to learn how the process has helped other people break free of limiting beliefs that kept them stuck in old patterns. A number of people have offered to share their success stories. I'm eager to hear yours, too!

Diane English — Artist, Author, Inspiration

"I can't imagine going back to my old paradigm of reality."

While artist/author/spiritual satirist Diane English was making people laugh with her Great Cosmic Happy-Ass creations, deep in her heart of hearts, she was terrified her popularity and success weren't real. Diane said she was frequently paralyzed with fear "... that I'm going to end up as a bag lady living under a bridge with a shopping cart full of second-hand canned goods and mismatched shoes. Oh yeah, and toothless."

When Diane finally put on the brakes and honestly observed her life to date, she realized that despite changes in her vocation, state of residence, relationships or fluctuating financial levels, none of her worst fears had ever been realized. In fact, her friends and growing legion of fans *constantly* praised her colorful, creative, thought-provoking work.

Diane obliterated her limiting beliefs the old fashioned way – she opened her heart and her mind to receive the kind words and compliments of others. This new empowering behavior immediately began melting away past blocks. She was also inspired by attending a few of my BOOM Thinking luncheons, where a delightfully eclectic group of businesswoman gather to be inspired and get connected with each other.

She consciously worked to create a new mindset by reading the spiritual works of Abraham-Hicks, Eckhart Tolle and Byron Katie, and listening to them on her MP3 player as she walked around a peaceful, pine tree-lined lake. "I immerse myself in their teachings,"

Diane said, "and it makes it so much easier to ignore the consensus reality and not get caught up in life-force sucking drama."

Results: Diane said she feels so much happier and freer, and she can't imagine going back to her old paradigm of reality. "I so much like playing, laughing and ignoring the drama that goes on in the world," she said. Another positive result is Diane's first book, "The Great Cosmic Happy-Ass Field Guide to Enlightenment," which is already in its second printing. Check out the book, and her other Happy-Ass offerings, at www.greatcosmichappyass.com.

Julie Parker: Magazine Editor, Website Designer

"My 'problems' became 'blessings.'"

Julie Parker, Publisher/Editor along with Sandi Tomlin-Sutker of Western North Carolina Woman magazine, has to keep a lot of balls in the air 24/7. Between planning, writing, editing and creating ads for the magazine which is distributed around the country, Julie is also the creator and head techie for her website design business, "Handwoven Webs." Her three canine kids constantly charge in and out of her home office, presenting further opportunities for distraction with each furry visit. The old mindset that Julie wanted to BOOM Think away was her habit of immediately reacting to negative situations instead of taking a step back, and looking at the intention or deeper meaning concerning the incident.

"For instance," Julie said, "I just got word that copies of the newest issue of the magazine were blowing around a busy city street. Before, I might have gone ballistic, but instead, I made some calls to find out what happened, and learned our delivery man's trunk wasn't latched shut. It's unfortunate, but certainly not an intentional or deliberate act. So there's nothing to get mad or complain about."

"The benefits of looking beyond what's happening on the surface are immediate and the process is actually fun," Julie said. She realizes now that the benefits of nurturing positive, proactive communication and follow-through are immensely more rewarding and beneficial than reactively getting mad when something goes wrong.

"The very first spiritual principle I learned back in the early 70s was from Maharishi Mahesh Yogi; 'That to which you give you attention grows stronger in your life,'" Julie said. "That was echoed by the teachings of Abraham (www.abraham-hicks.com) that I came across 10 years ago, and most recently, *The Secret*. So the seed was planted more than 30 years ago and has been growing ever since. I just applied some very powerful fertilizer in the last couple of years."

Julie said her main challenge is to catch herself when she starts to complain, and remind herself, "In the grand scheme of life, this is piddly."

One tool she employed was a bracelet from the website www.acomplaintfreeworld.org. "There it sits, on your wrist, kind of annoying, as I am not used to wearing a bracelet...*not that I am complaining*!" Julie joked. "Kind of hard to complain when there is that constant reminder right there!" (Snap!)

Julie also occasionally "zooms out" on her life and looks at it from afar, as if she was a character in a novel, and sees it in perspective.

Results: Her positive benefits from the BOOM Thinking process were immediate and measurable, Julie reported. "'Problems,' things I might have complained about in the past, seem insignificant," she said. "'Problems' become blessings."

Find out more about Julie's progress, her work, and her blessings on her websites at www.wncwoman.com and www.handwovenwebs.com.

Sandi Tomlin-Sutker: Editor, Entrepreneur

"The past does NOT predict the future!"

Still sporting the long, straight hair and flowing peasant skirts from her hippie 60's days, Sandi Tomlin-Sutker, the other half of the brilliant Western North Carolina Magazine editing/publishing team, frequently got caught up in old fear-based thinking.

"When it was time to pay the bills, and there wasn't enough money in the checking account to pay them, it was a challenge to feel confident that the money would **be there** exactly when I needed it," Sandi said. "Or, if my husband and I were not in a good place with each other, it was a challenge," she added. For Sandi, putting on the brakes and observing meant remembering that her perceptions of reality and her attitude toward her marriage, or anything, for that matter, are responsible for how the situation feels and looks at any point in time.

To obliterate old fears and move into a positive new mindset, Sandi set out in a positive new direction. She started devouring positive intention literature; listening to inspirational tapes, going to empowering presentations and workshops – anything, she said, to help her break free of the old mental habits of fear and anxiety. She also decided to remember to trust herself and her instincts – the same instincts that had safely guided her through decades of growth and change.

Results: "I feel better, happier, and more trusting in the process of my life," Sandi said. "I have more money coming in, I have new prospects for income appearing all the time now, and my husband and I are going to Ireland for our 30th wedding anniversary this summer!" Amid the happy flurry of activity now that fills her days, if she ever falls back into those limiting old beliefs, she has more evidence and support to help her shift quickly.

"How things look today says *nothing* about how they will look tomorrow," Sandi said. "What I see right now is just one moment in time, and tomorrow is a different moment. This relates to money issues and to relationship issues as well." Read more of Sandi's reflections in her articles posted on her website at www.wncwoman.com.

> *Let the world know you as you are, not as you think you should be, because sooner or later, if you are posing, you will forget the pose, and then where are you?*
>
> *- Fanny Brice*

Tena Frank: *Real Estate Developer*

"The Universe will give me what I ask for."

When Tena Frank launched her career as a social worker, becoming a real estate developer was about the furthest thing from her mind. It wasn't that she didn't have big ideas – she just tussled with the limiting mindset that she was doomed to a life of being "all idea and no action."

"I have really huge ideas - and they often come to me spontaneously and full blown," Tena said. What limiting belief held her hostage? "The terrible triad: Procrastination, Perfectionism and Frustration!

I have all the excuses that everyone else has for not getting things done and for not trying to bring my ideas into actuality: I don't have the time, I don't have the knowledge or the skill, it isn't really all that important, I don't want to, I can't, I'll do it later.

"Another piece of the problem for me is the really deep belief that I have to do it all myself; that there is no one who is interested or willing to help me. So that huge, wonderful idea languishes."

After decades of feeling "stuck," Tena was able to BOOM Think her way out of her rut by engaging with her spirituality.

"I have had a strong sense of connection to the Universe my whole life," Tena explained, "but I always experienced this connection more as a source of *inspiration* than as a source of *action*. Somewhere along the line I forgot what I knew as a kid: The Universe will give me what I ask for. I didn't have a name for it until I began working with Cheri and she told me about the Law of Attraction."

Tena was struck by a sign I have hanging on my wall that says **She believed she could, so she did.** "That simple thought really opened my eyes," Tena said, "and I quickly realized that when I say 'I can't', I'm right. And when I say 'I can', I'm right!'" In her new mindset, Tena consciously worked to stay in a positive frame of mind, and she also embraced the liberating idea of "teamwork."

Results: *"*When I first began the BOOM Thinking process, I owned some property that has great potential for development, but I knew virtually nothing about how to do it," Tena said. "Instead of letting my vision die on the vine, I went about creating a development team. I found an architect, a land planner and a construction company. I'd have to say that being willing to take risks is also one of the strategies I've used to make positive changes in my life."

Besides being well on her way to becoming a real estate tycoon, Tena's finished a rough draft of her first novel, renovated her house and learned how to trade stock options. "I'm taking a 9-day trip with friends into the Peruvian Amazon in the spring," Tena laughed. "It's something I would *never* have given a second thought in the past. By challenging the way I used to think, I've become more productive and happier."

Ana Tampana: Life Coach and Author

"I am seeing the universality and connectedness of the human condition."

For Ana Tampana, a series of calamitous family events left her grief-stricken, angry and financially crippled. "I *left* a career I had worked hard to develop so that I could be home to nurture hurting family members," Ana said. "At times, I had to wade through extreme depression and fear that I couldn't provide for my family. I felt unbridled anger towards people who had victimized family members. Sometimes, I felt victimized by the family members themselves since I was the buffer for their emotional outbursts." Besides having to deal with her own grief at the murder of her daughter-in-law, her husband's subsequent job layoff and a string of other overwhelming events, Ana was battling the limiting belief that she would never be successful or prosperous.

Ana began to crawl out of her rut when she came to the understanding that, "The world doesn't 'stop and wait' for me to handle emergencies, then return where I left off. I also had to realize that neither my spouse nor I was financially educated, and if there was to be real development in this area, it was up to me."

Ana's process for breaking out of limiting mindsets was disciplined and focused. First, she journaled daily, writing down her negative thoughts and fears, then responding to them with what she knew was really true. "I worked through forgiveness processes whenever I found myself feeling angry or resentful," Ana said. "I also volunteered after every disaster or tragedy. This helped me stay focused on what I could give to someone else, putting me in an empowered mindset. It also led to new friendships, and experiences of the heart. There is

ALWAYS someone dealing with a situation much worse than mine. Many times, the person on the receiving end of my services inspired me with his or her courage."

She shifted to focusing on affirming other people, exercising daily, reconnecting with old friends, taking financial planning workshops and tithing at church, even when it meant sometimes only giving a dollar.

Results: "I am seeing the universality and connectedness of the human condition," Ana said. "There are people hurting and paralyzed with fear everywhere. But, truly, tragedy and adversity build character. It strips a person to the very core of who he or she is. My faith became stronger. Even life threatening disease allows a new aspect of oneself to show up. One becomes acquainted with one's inner strength like never before. Humor becomes a valuable tool."

"I have become very committed to social justice. My values provide my motivation rather than my ego now, and my focus is razor sharp. I am more determined than ever." This woman who was at one point "up to her butt in alligators" is now "The Alligator Coach," using her own challenges to motivate and inspire others. Check out her website, www.alligatorcoach.com.

Lynne Harty: *Photographer and Visionary*

"New creative projects are literally falling in my lap."

The nagging fear that she couldn't create anything that anyone would want to buy was the limiting belief that made photographer Lynne Harty shudder. "I had trouble believing in my own creativity," she said.

Lynne peeped out of her rut long enough to realize she had to change things in her life if she was going to make it, and she decided to enroll in a BOOM Thinking workshop.

"Taking your class was enormously helpful," Lynne said. "It was also incredibly helpful to me to have the support from the group. I'm convinced that is what propelled me to actually produce the new work."

Results: After Lynne developed the confidence to pitch her creative work to prospective clients, everything in her life changed. Her series, "Asheville – a Contemporary View," opened at local gallery and store Mobilia to rave reviews, and was featured in an Asheville arts magazine. The city's Chamber of Commerce put Lynne's work in its 2007 Visitor's Guide, Asheville Magazine, and the Chamber's Membership Recruitment guide.

"New creative projects are literally falling in my lap these days," Lynne laughed. "It's just amazing." Take a look at Lynne's work on her website, www.lynneharty.com.

> *The important thing is this: To be able at any moment to sacrifice what we are for what we could become.*
>
> *~ Charles Dubois*

Lincoln Crum: *Real Estate Broker and Entrepreneur*

"I finally decided that 'someday' is NOW!"

For 20 years Lincoln Crum was in real estate, and for 20 years he'd been squandering his knowledge, expertise and creative ideas while his bank balance languished.

"I was great at giving free advice, and setting up fantastic deals for other people while they took all the credit," Lincoln said. It wasn't until last year, after his company engaged me to do a teleconference for the Realtors, that Lincoln realized he'd fallen into the rut of the nice guy finishing last – last in commissions, last in recognition, and last in opportunities to take ownership of his career and his finances.

"Cheri made me realize I did this to myself, and I had to break out of this old mindset," Lincoln said. "I finally saw that I wasn't valuing myself enough. Here I was handing out advice and ideas that made other people rich, and I hadn't tied my contributions to any real income. A pat on the back is *nice*, but it doesn't pay my mortgage or feed my kids."

After he recognized this limiting pattern, Lincoln began BOOM Thinking in earnest. "I became consciously aware of what I was doing at all times, and I started saying 'no,' or asking how we could tie a value to my contribution," Lincoln said. "A long-time client wanted me to put a deal together for him, and he would reap all the benefits. Previously I would have done that for him – but this time, I refused." Ironically, as Lincoln began standing up for himself, his clients gained new respect for him.

Results: These days, Lincoln is structuring his own deals, and reaping the financial rewards that are putting him well on his way to achieving financial abundance in 2008. "I always said that I was going to make it 'someday,'" Lincoln said, "and I finally decided that 'someday' is NOW!" He's still a nice guy, he insists – it's just that now, this is one nice guy who's no longer the last to be rewarded. He knows his contributions have value, and he's finally collecting on that! Visit Lincoln's website at www.reallivingrightnow.com.

Caren Olmsted: Artist

"I give myself permission to be joyful!"

A visit to Caren's website at www.cfodesign.com shows a beaming, luminous woman holding one of her signature creations – a guitar transformed into a functional work of art. The joy and confidence emanating from the photo, however, is a relatively *new* mindset for Caren.

"Before, I really had a great deal of fear," Caren admitted. "I was afraid my artwork was not valuable or worthy. I had deep fear of rejection, fear of failure, fear that people wouldn't like it, fear that there wouldn't be enough work. FEAR, FEAR, FEAR!"

Despite her initial hesitation, Caren couldn't ignore her 'inner artist,' and battled her limiting beliefs on several fronts. Affirmations were just the beginning.

"I also did the Artist's Way," Caren said. "Using the morning pages to highlight and clarify my limiting beliefs really shown a light on how untrue a lot of my beliefs were." Caren followed through with group and individual coaching sessions, vision boards, and… belly dancing!

"The movement of belly dancing helped my art in unbelievable ways," Caren said. "I also consciously created an intentional community, full of loving, supportive people."

Results: "When I go to work now," Caren said, "I feel free, loved and joyful because I give myself permission to be so! I know that it is OK for me to make some mistakes; to 'fail' on occasion. I also now usually avoid situations and people where I know I will encounter negativity. When I can't, then I use affirmations and my 'people' to help me navigate though!" Take a virtual tour of Caren's CFO Design gallery at www.cfodesign.com.

Patricia Dee: Financial and Life Coach

"Your 'value' has nothing to do with your checkbook!"

By all outward appearances, Patricia Dee was on top of the world. Through hard work, sheer determination and her highly-polished professional skill set, Patricia had scaled the highest peaks of the cut-throat banking and financial industry to achieve monetary abundance, prestige, power, and tons of material "stuff."

Deep inside her gold-lined rut, however, Patricia's psyche was possessed by the shame-driven mantra, "If I *have* nothing, then I AM nothing." She learned this negative belief from her father early on, and it had driven her throughout her childhood, schooling and career to overachieve at any cost.

"The early signs of trouble came in the form of a failing marriage, a breast tumor, and a series of disputes with superiors and a Board of Directors," Patricia said. "One wanted me to lie, the other to conceal the truth, and I refused and fought back." The fallout and betrayal that resulted from Patricia refusing to compromise her ethics eventually led to her being pressured out of those two jobs, feeling exiled from the Boston financial industry and fleeing the big city life and a soul-sucking approach to career to pursue her spiritual path in North Carolina.

At first Patricia believed that immersing herself in nontraditional therapies, prayer, and positive thought was all she needed to do to heal. "I still did not understand the even greater power of a deeply held, unconscious, emotionally charged belief that said to me that I was NOTHING and deserved NOTHING because I had nothing," Patricia said. "This limiting belief told me I had lost everything of true value."

The shame of having to file for bankruptcy was the last straw, but also the genesis for Patricia getting back in balance with the Universe. She was shocked to finally realize that her entire belief in herself had been based on material wealth. When the friends and family members who had only valued Patricia's financial success beat a hasty retreat, she moved into a BOOM Thinking mode. "I made it my mission to find all of those things that I liked about myself and my life and to celebrate them," Patricia said. "I realized I was bringing myself up as a newborn, and only I could really make myself believe I had value outside of money and achievement. I surrounded myself with people who would affirm my true value and stopped focusing on what I did not have."

Results: Patricia channeled her business and financial skills into restoring her financial health. "I looked at my numbers, set income goals and deadlines, actions steps I would have to take. I made a plan to eventually earn my living combining what I liked, what I was good at, and what was most marketable. I resolved to spend my money on only those things that bring me the greatest satisfaction. I had a plan to get there so it no longer felt hopeless and endless."

In the process, Patricia realized lots of others would profit from a similar self-evaluation and redirection, and she has put her years of experience and her MBA to work in creating a financial consulting and coaching business to help others benefit from her skills, past mistakes and current growth. "My struggle is part of my gift to others," she said. Visit her website at www.seedstrategies.com.

Tools for Building a
BOOMing Life

"It's not so much
that we're afraid
of change or so
in love with the
old ways, but
it's that place in
between that we
fear . . . . It's like
being between
trapezes. It's
Linus when his
blanket is in the
dryer. There's
nothing to hold
on to."
~ Marilyn
Ferguson

Chapter 10

Chapter 10

Tools for Building a BOOMING Life!

Now that we've covered the nuts and bolts of BOOM Thinking, I'm wrapping up by sharing some resources that will help you successfully:

- Put on the **B**rakes,

- **O**bserve what's happening in your life,

- **O**bliterate the limiting beliefs and habits that are no longer serving you, and

- **M**ake a new Mindset.

1. Community

You've heard the saying that a single twig is easily broken, while a bundle of twigs is strong. Make it a priority to cultivate friendships with like-minded people who can share with you their support, camaraderie and experience. The minute I shifted from hanging out with perfect parents with perfect kids and cultivated friendships with other families whose children also had learning disabilities like my own kids, my life changed for the better.

For myself, and for many of the clients I work with, there are some beliefs I've been able to shift relatively easily. In other cases, I've needed a multi-pronged approach. I need to elicit the support of friends; I need some therapy, some good books, sticky notes all over the house, and a mantra of the way I want to think to create a new path for my wheelbarrow. That really requires a strong, close-knit network of allies. A supportive community can make all the difference in the world in your success with both identifying and then shifting old limiting beliefs.

2. Assemble a Strong Support Team

One of the biggest mistakes people make is thinking they have to cover all the bases of their business or their life single-handedly. Let's just squelch that absurd mindset once and for all. There are many aspects of your personal and professional life that you handle with talent, confidence and ease. Then there are the other aspects, where your best effort is like trimming a hedge with your tweezers. Sometimes the old adage, "The right tools for the job," refers to people power. Look for the people whose skill sets compliment your own.

Identify the characteristics of the people who could support your goals. Don't think in terms of specific individuals because they might not turn out to be the best ones for the task. Instead, list the key skills you're looking for in a person and include that information in your plan.

3. Forgiveness

In the course of your life and your career, people are going to step on your toes, and you're going to make some gargantuan miscalculations, misjudgments and missteps yourself. Get over it. Forgive your trespassers, and yourself, and move on. Learn from your mistakes so you don't repeat them, but know that you're statistically going to have many more failures than successes.

Thomas Edison created nearly 5,000 light bulbs that *didn't* work before he found the one design that did. Now, 130 years later, his invention is still lighting up our world. If he had castigated himself for his many, many unsuccessful attempts instead of being forgiving, we'd all be watching TV by candlelight.

4. Gratitude

For centuries, spiritually enlightened beings have told us that living in an attitude of gratitude is powerful and healing. This millennium, traditional science has finally caught up. Robert A. Emmons, a psychology professor at the University of California, Davis, has accumulated data that actually proves expressing gratitude makes you healthier, smarter and more energetic.

Even when you're bopped on the head by a BOOM Boomerang, like we mentioned in Chapter 5, you can express gratitude that you have this new opportunity to learn and grow. Make gratitude a habit. You'll thank yourself!

5. Laughter

Finally, one of the most effective ways we do this work is with lightness and levity. When we can look at ourselves and our human foibles without harsh judgments, it's so freeing. Even if you don't always get to pick your circumstances, you definitely always get to pick your reaction to those circumstances. Why not pick humor? Just like the recently proven health benefits of expressing gratitude, similar benefits from laughter have been recognized in the Western medical community for decades. In one of the most well-known cases, writer Norman Cousins laughed himself free of cancer by watching slapstick movies and TV shows. Now, *that's* funny.

BOOM Book List

There's a bit of BOOM Thinking in each of the following books, and I heartily recommend *all* of them:

Comfort Secrets for Busy Women: Finding Your Way When Your Life Is Overflowing by Jennifer Louden (Harmony Books, 2000)

In my well-worn copy of this book, I've written about as much in the margins as Jennifer did in the book. She is my mentor, my life coach, my cheerleader and my inspiration. Just thumbing through this treasure chest of ideas propels me into a happier universe.

The Life Organizer: Tips, Stories, & Prompts to Focus on Your Needs & Navigate Your Dreams by Jennifer Louden (New World Library, 2006)

In this book, Jennifer's turned each week into an opportunity for deep introspection and celebration of the project that is your life. It's a colorful, richly detailed book that helps you focus not only on getting tasks done but how you want to "be" as you're living your life.

How to be HAPPY, Dammit: A Cynic's Guide to Spiritual Happiness by Karen Salmansohn (Celestial Arts, 2001)

This colorful, yummy bon-bon of a book simultaneously made me laugh and think, and I just loved it. A little silly, a little science, a little introspection, and a *lot* of encouragement blend seamlessly into an inspiring read that will have you jumping out of your chair and eager to take on the world.

A Little Book on the Human Shadow by Robert Bly (Harper San Francisco, 1988)

I already referenced this powerful little book back in Chapter Six. Everyone has a shadow side; don't be kept in the dark.

A Short Guide to a Happy Life by Anna Quindlen (Random House, 2000)

What started as a commencement speech has become a runaway bestseller, and for a very good reason. Anna gets to the heart of what really matters, and I faithfully read this inspiring message every six months — at least!

Parenting with Love and Logic: Teaching Children Responsibility
by Foster Cline, M.D. & Jim Fay (Pinion Press, 1990)

Like most mothers, my initial instinct was to wrap my kids in an impenetrable cocoon of overprotection and suffocating love. And then life happened. The authors show us how more balanced approaches, where we give the kids less in life, actually result in our children getting more out of everything.

Take Time for Your Life by Cheryl Richardson (Broadway Books, 1998)

Cheryl talks about creating the life you want, and she's one of the big inspirations that helped me develop BOOM Thinking.

Attracting Perfect Customers: The Power of Strategic Synchronicity by Stacey Hall & Jan Brogniez (Berrett-Koehler Publishers, Inc., 2001)

What would happen if you stopped thinking about growing your business as a "battle" and instead saw it as an opportunity to attract *exactly* the types of folks you'd like to have in your life? Stacey and Jan helped me transform the way I run both my personal and professional lives.

Circle of Stones: Woman's Journey to Herself by Judith Duerk
(LauraMedia, 1989)

> Judith suggests the idea that a strong, supportive network of
> women to guide and nurture you throughout your life might
> have made a huge difference. It's inspired me to extend my
> hand to other women, too.

The Great Cosmic Happy-Ass Field Guide to Enlightenment by
Diane English (Self-published, 2007)

> Irreverent, politically incorrect and hysterically funny, this full-
> color jewel of a first book is packed with Diane's cartoons and
> off-beat wisdom. It inspires, reaffirms, ridicules and tickles
> your fancy.

The Dark Side of the Light Chasers by Debbie Ford (Riverhead
Books, 1998)

> When we have the courage to honestly examine what we
> *think* are our weaknesses, we can find our true strengths
> and live authentically. Debbie's the one who shares the
> great concept of "inner critics" getting on your metaphorical
> school bus to travel through life with you, second-guessing
> everything you think, say or do.

Eat, Pray, Love by Elizabeth Gilbert (Penguin Books, 2006)

I just loved everything about this delicious book. Elizabeth's pain, confusion, hopes, fears, dreams and ultimately her heart's desire are splayed upon each and every page with no apology. It's a feast for the senses and a powerful example of what can happen when you purposefully obliterate your old ways of approaching your life and create something entirely new.

The Glass Castle by Jeanette Walls (Scribner, 2006)

This heart-wrenching and simultaneously inspiring story is one woman's memoir of a lifetime of BOOM Thinking. When her brilliant and deeply flawed parents weren't up to the task of raising Jeanette and her brother, the kids raised themselves, with phenomenal success.

New and Selected Poems by Mary Oliver (Beacon Press, 1992)

Although every selection created powerful images in my mind, "The Journey" imprinted itself on my heart. Read it and weep — seriously!

A Primer in Positive Psychology by Christopher Peterson (Oxford University Press, 2006)

> This is the definitive textbook on what goes right in people's lives by one of the respected leaders in this relatively new field. For years psychologists just studied what made people depressed. Thanks to innovators like Chris, now more therapists are studying what makes people *happy*. Bravo!!

Excuse Me, Your Life Is Waiting: The Astonishing Power of Feelings by Lynn Grabhorn (Hampton Roads, 2000)

> By now, the principle of the Power of Attraction is well known, but Lynn was one of the pioneers sounding the trumpet that what we feel and think about is what we bring into our lives. It's a little book with a big attitude, and it definitely transformed how I viewed my life!

A Woman's Field Guide to Exceptional Living by Corrie Woods (Morgan James Publishing, 2007)

> Corrie is a friend and coaching client, and she brings a grounded yet playful sense of wonder to everything she does. This book encourages women to not settle for a lackluster life but to live on all cylinders and celebrate their uniqueness.

Boom Links

Check out the following websites for some more juicy BOOM Thinking ideas.

Christinekane.com: Christine is a fabulous songwriter and singer. She not only touches people through her music but also through her incredible blog. She encourages us all to "Be creative, Be conscious, Be courageous."

Mollygordon.com: Molly is an incredible coach. This website is stuffed full of ideas and resources that help you live a full and thriving life…including doing work that feeds your soul.

Tut.com: This website is dedicated to helping others understand that thoughts become things…so choose the good ones. You can sign up here to receive a daily e-mail from the Universe directly to you. These emails are among my favorite ways to start my day.

Abraham-hicks.com: A fabulous resource to learn more about the teachings from Abraham in dialogues with Ester Hicks. Great resource.

Comfortqueen.com: I've already raved about my friend Jennifer. Check her out. You can also read her blog at www.jenniferlouden.com.

Howmuchjoy.com: Suzanne Falter-Barnes helps you reach out and find your joy. Go for it!

GreatCosmicHappyAss.com: Allow some time to poke around this great website. Diane's irreverent yet profound sense of humor will have you laughing, thinking, sending e-cards to your friends and feeling oh-so-good.

Thework.com: This is the website where Byron Katie, author and spiritual teacher, helps people heal their own suffering. She is the creator of "The Work." If you know about the work, and even if you don't yet, check it out. This is powerful stuff!

Monihill.com: Moni Hill, the talented woman who created custom illustrations for this book, has dozens of great designs on her website. Take the tour. It's really tweet.

Happymedium.us: Besides working on books, my editor, Jonna Rae, is a Happy Medium. She sees dead people so you don't have to.

"*Remember no
one can make
you feel inferior
without your
consent.*"

*–Eleanor
Roosevelt*

Sasha Has the Last Word

pilogue

Epilogue

Sasha Has the Last Word

(Editor's Note: Help! Sasha has wrestled control of the computer from Cheri and is beginning to type RIGHT NOW! HELP!...)

Well!

You just *had* to go and read this book, didn't you? Now how do you think your *own* inner critics are going to find work?

You're probably going to BOOM Think away their constant criticism about the things you say and do, their ridicule toward your ambitious goals and their catty put-downs for the way you look and dress, aren't you?

Well just remember *this* — if it hadn't been for our vicious, nagging voices in your head, you probably wouldn't have been motivated to change those old behaviors that kept you firmly entrenched in the "just-getting-by" lane!

As for me, I plan to drop in on Cheri now and then, probably mainly around the holidays. I know she'll just BOOM me away, but I don't want her to get too comfortable and start to settle for that velvet rut again.

I am very proud that I was able to keep Cheri from writing this book for many years! Between you and me, she didn't really talk about the times I won — and I'm extremely disappointed those times are getting fewer and farther between. But did you notice the book's illustrations aren't in color, and it's not hardcover? Hummmmm?

Meanwhile, I'm getting on with my life. I'm working on getting booked on Oprah. I'm going to reveal to the whole world how unfair it is that you're all reading books like this, BOOM Thinking us inner critics out of your lives, and putting us out of a job. Sure, Oprah's obliterated an army of us already, but maybe if I ask her why she and Steadman aren't married yet, or what size she's wearing these days, she'll let me stick around a bit and work on her…

ABOUT THE EDITOR
Jonna Rae Bartges of Bartges Communication

When Jonna Rae was born, her parents decided that would be a good "pen name" for her, and she's been writing ever since. The Emmy award-winner launched her career as a newspaper journalist and television news producer before jumping into the communications and marketing arena. She's logged time in major TV markets like Los Angeles and Miami, and she also headed up PR efforts for Disneyland, Sea World and LEGOLAND California. Some of her marketing coups include getting Entertainment Tonight's Leonard Maltin to interview George Lucas on the Indiana Jones ride at Disneyland, landing one billion documented media impressions for LEGOLAND the year it opened, and making Sea World's rehabilitation and release of an orphaned gray whale calf a National Geographic special and live CNN report. She's featured in the book, *The Marketer's Guide to Public Relations in the 21st Century* by Thomas L. Harris and Patricia T. Whalen.

She's also a prolific writer and editor, with numerous magazine articles and several books to her credit. Contact her through her website at www.bartges.com.

ABOUT THE ILLUSTRATOR
Moni Hill of Be Tweet Productions®

Moni Hill was born in Germany and raised in Cincinnati, Ohio. She earned a degree in Political Science from Hiram College in Hiram, Ohio and eventually found her way to the hills of Appalachia in 1996 when she moved to Charlottesville, Virginia to be with her (now) husband, whom she met whitewater rafting in West Virginia. After a couple of moves up and down the

Appalachian Mountains and two children later, they've landed in Asheville, North Carolina. And boy, are they glad!

Moni has been an artist all of her life, but her passion for creating vibrant pieces of art blossomed once she quit her corporate jobs and began spending time in mountains, on rivers, and in gardens. Now her art pours out of her thanks to the endless supply of inspiration from the beauty of her natural surroundings, the joy of her children, and the spirit and culture of the Appalachian Mountains. As a wife and mother of two young daughters, she tends to get caught up in a whirlwind of activities and lose perspective on life. Painting transforms her anxieties into colorful expressions of what she is aiming for in her inner life: stillness, authenticity, gratitude, beauty and joy. Check out her gallery exhibits and contact her through her website at www.monihill.com.

ABOUT THE AUTHOR
Cheri Britton, M.Ed.

Cheri has been helping individuals and organizations effectively BOOM Think for over two decades. She is an author, professional speaker, coach and trainer, and she conveys her empowering message through metaphors and engaging anecdotes taken from her vibrant personal life. She's committed to reinvigorating business owners, executives, employees, entrepreneurs and regular folks with her gutsy, gritty approach to facing obstacles head on and transforming them into positive opportunities for growth, success and fulfillment.

She is also the President and CEO of Whetstone Consultations, a consulting business that works specifically with healthcare agencies.

As a single mom raising two youngsters, Cheri maintains a realistic view of working professionals who juggle careers with family and outside interests. She earned a Masters Degree in Education from the University of North Carolina at Charlotte and is an active member of the National Speakers Association. Cheri resides in Asheville, North Carolina with her two children and her dogs, Boomer, Moxie and Chance. Visit her website at www.boomthinking.com.

BOOM

Break Out of Old Mindsets

Thinking™

WANT TO KNOW MORE ABOUT
BOOM THINKING™?

Learn more about BOOM Thinking™
by visiting www.boomthinking.com.

Can you image a world full of BOOM thinkers, where individuals,
families, communities, businesses, large corporations, even
governments and whole countries were willing to break out of old
limiting mindsets?

I believe it's possible.
And you know how we get there?
One new thought, one small change, one brave shift at a time.

Are you willing to be a BOOM Thinker and help change the world?

Who are you **NOT** to?

At www.boomthinking.com read other people's stories about how
BOOM Thinking is transforming things. We invite you to share
your story too.